THE OFFICIAL MOTORCYCLE HANDBOOK

FOR MOTORCYCLE DRIVERS

This booklet is only a guide. For official purposes, please refer to the Highway Traffic Act and the Off-Road Vehicles Act of Ontario and Regulations.

Note: Instructions for driving and handling of a motorcycle in this handbook are only advisory. Drivers should exercise their own judgement in any given situation.

Disponible en français
Demandez le «Guide officiel des motocyclettes»

Driving is a privilege—not a right

Introduction

This handbook has been prepared as a guide to safe riding techniques and practices and as a guide to Ontario's laws regarding the use of motorcycles. The Driver's Handbook must be used along with this handbook.

Motorcycling can be an exhilarating experience. Yet it can also be a dangerous one unless the riding task is taken seriously.

In 1993, motorcycles comprised 1.8 per cent of all registered motor vehicles. While the number of fatalities have been declining over the past few years, motorcycle drivers and passengers represent 5.2 per cent of all fatalities.

Of all motorcycle drivers in fatal collisions, 46 per cent were under the age of 25. Approximately 58 per cent of the errors attributable to the motorcycle driver in fatal collisions were speed too fast, or lost control. Of the drivers in fatal collisions, 15 per cent were incorrectly licensed for the vehicle.

It should be remembered that a motorcycle is one of the smallest vehicles on the road and drivers and passengers are vulnerable in the event of a collision. To survive, a motorcyclist must drive defensively.

Every novice driver, or someone wishing to improve their skills should take a motorcycle training course.

A course may offer you many things:

■ personal instruction from experts
■ a motorcycle provided for about 14 hours of practice
■ riding test for your Class M2 driver's licence
■ valuable tips and skills to keep you safe on the road
■ the possibility of an insurance discount on your bike (check with your insurance company)

If you would like more information about motorcycle driver training, or a course being conducted near you, call your local community college, local Ministry Driver Examination Centre, or this toll-free number: 1-800-267-6292.

Contents

Introduction   2
Becoming an expert motorcyclist   4

Chapter 1

Driver licence information   5
Class M1   6
Class M2   6
Vehicle licence information   7
Off-road vehicles   7
Skill test   8
On street riding demonstration   9
Motorcycle equipment
Requirements   10
Safety standards certificate   12
Buying or selling a used vehicle 12
Being in shape to drive your bike 13

Chapter 2

Preparing to drive   15
The helmet   15
Eye and face protection   16
Protective clothing   16
Know your motorcycle controls 18
Daily motorcycle check   24

Chapter 3

Precision—learning to control a
motorcycle like an expert   27
Body position   27
Turning   28
Braking   29
Shifting gears   29

Chapter 4

Being aware and alert   31
Checking the road surface   33
Using mirrors   33
Learning to anticipate   34
Headlight   34
Clothing   35
Nighttime visibility   35
Lane position   36
Horn   36
Signalling   36
Brake light   37
Eye contact   37
Left turn in front of motorcycle 38

Chapter 5

Position—learning your place

on the road   39
Lane position—blocking   39
Position for turning   41
Circle of safety   43
Distance in front   44
Two-second rule   44
Distance to the side   45
Passing vehicles   45
Parked cars   46
Lane changes   46
Sharing lanes   47
Distance behind   48
Position for seeing   49
Position for being seen   51
Group riding   53
Riding at night   55
Handling dangerous surfaces 56
Riding in bad weather   60
Emergencies   62
Carrying passengers and cargo 67
Accessories and modifications 69
Maintenance   70
Could you pass?   72

Chapter 6   73

Becoming an expert motorcyclist

In Ontario, you are required to have a Class M driver's licence to drive a motorcycle on the streets and highways. This handbook will provide you with information, knowledge and skills you'll need while learning to be a safe and expert driver.

Information on motorcycle licensing and laws on their operation in Ontario are contained on pages 5-11.

The handbook includes information on getting ready to drive your bike, covering such areas as proper clothing, helmet regulations, knowing your motorcycle and controls.

Riding a bike well takes a lot of practice and experience. You must know where to drive in your lane; how to react to the mistakes of other drivers; how to see like an expert and be seen by other motorists; how to handle dangerous surfaces and emergencies.

To drive well, you must be in good physical and mental condition, because handling a motorcycle demands more concentration and is more tiring than driving a car.

The drinking driver is a serious problem, especially among motorcycle drivers. Alcohol seriously affects the mind and body. This is why so many motorcyclists who have been drinking, end up killed or disabled for life.

Drivers may find carrying passengers or cargo is more demanding than riding a bike alone and this text explains what to watch for when there are two on a bike.

The skills and procedures discussed in this handbook, together with your learning experiences on your motorcycle, can help you meet the challenges of operating on our streets and highways. What you learn will add to the pleasure that riding your bike can provide.

DRIVER LICENCE INFORMATION

As of April 1, 1994, new drivers applying for their first car or motorcycle licence enter Ontario's graduated licensing system. Under graduated licensing, new drivers gain driving experience and skills gradually. It is a two-step licensing process that takes a minimum of 20 months to complete.

To apply for a Level One motorcycle licence, you must be at least 16 years old and pass a vision test and a test of your knowledge of the rules of the road. You must also pass a written test of your knowledge of motorcycles. After you pass these tests you will receive a Class M1 licence and a novice driver information package.

During the licensing process, you must pass two road tests. The first road test is necessary to move to Level Two (Class M2) and the second road test is necessary to graduate to full driving privileges and your Class M licence.

Motorcycle licence requirements

Here are the rules you must follow at each level of the Class M licensing process:

Level One (Class M1)

Level One lasts a minimum of 60 days and the Level One licence is valid for 90 days.

At Level One:

- You must not drive if you have been drinking alcohol. Your blood alcohol level must be zero.
- You must drive only during daylight hours — one-half hour before sunrise to one-half hour after sunset.
- You must not drive on highways with speed limits of more than 80 km/h except highways 11, 17, 61, 69, 71, 101, 102, 144, 655. (These exceptions are made because some drivers have no lower-speed routes available to them.)
- You must not carry passengers.
- You must pass a road test of your driving skills before being eligible to proceed to Level Two. At this time, you will be given a Class M2 licence. (See pages 8 and 9 for a description of the first road test.)

Please note: If you take your Level One test as part of a recognized motorcycle safety course, you must still wait the 60 days to move to Level Two.

Level Two (Class M2)

Level Two lasts a minimum of 22 months for motorcycle drivers. You may reduce your Level Two time requirement by four months by completing an approved motorcycle safety course. This course can be taken in Level One or Level Two. At Level Two, you gain many more privileges — you may now drive at night and on any road.

However, at Level Two:

- You must not drive if you have been drinking alcohol. Your blood alcohol level must be zero.

You will be eligible to take a comprehensive road test after you have completed the time required at Level Two. You must pass this test to get a Class M licence. For more information about the Level Two road test, see chapter 6.

Class M2 and Class M licence holders may also drive Class G vehicles under the conditions that apply to a Class G1 licence holder.

Please see The Official Driver's Handbook for more information on Class G licensing.

Licence combinations

Any class or combination of licence classes from "G" to "A" may be combined with Class "M1" or "M2", authorizing the operation of motorcycles if the applicant meets the requirements for Class "M". Additional authorization would be indicated by the combination of the licence class designation, i.e. "GM", "AM",

"EM", "ABM", "GM2", "AM2", "EM2", "ABM2".

Vehicle licence information

Licence plates are required for motorcycles when driven on public roads. Ontario has compulsory motor vehicle insurance. A written declaration of insurance coverage must be presented before you can register a vehicle, or renew a vehicle registration.

Under the Ontario vehicle registration system, your annual validation sticker expires on your birthday. It must be renewed prior to your motorcycle being operated on a highway.

Own choice plates are available from your local licence issuing office for a fee. Motorcycles may have 2-5 characters. If owners choose all numerals, they may select as few as 2 or as many as 4 in any combination.

Off-road vehicles

The Off-Road Vehicles Act, and regulations govern the operation of off-road vehicles in Ontario. As far as motorcyclists are concerned, this legislation covers vehicles used off-road, such as trail bikes. For further information refer to MTO's Official Off-Road Vehicles Handbook.

Motorcycle skill test manoeuvres for Class M1

For this 3-part motorcycle skill test, sets of 2 cones placed 1 metre apart, with each set being 5 metres apart, are used to test the applicant's skill in manoeuvring the vehicle.

The following is an explanation of each part:

Walk test (Figure "8"): Walk the motorcycle around the cones in a figure "8", preferably with both hands on the hand grips. Without losing control or dropping the bike, the applicant must stop the motorcycle with the front wheel on the stop line at the end of the Figure "8".

Serpentine drive: While moving slowly and keeping both feet on the foot rests during the test, the applicant must drive through the serpentine in a controlled manner.

Straight line brake test: While moving slowly and keeping both feet on the foot rests during the test, the applicant must drive in a straight line between the rows of cones, turn while remaining in control, accelerate in preparation for the brake test and then bring the motorcycle to a quick, safe, controlled stop with the front wheel on the start-finish line.

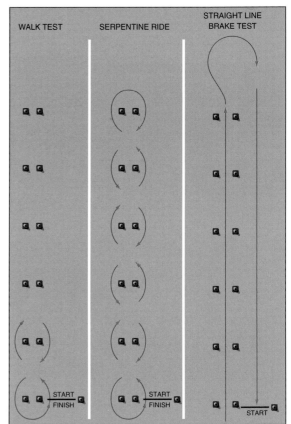

Diagram 1-1

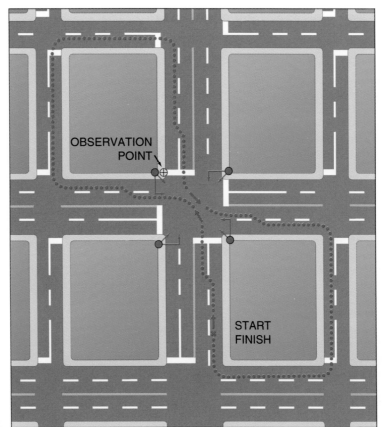

On-street riding demonstration

This illustration shows a typical on-street riding route used at the Ministry Driver Examination Centres across the province that give motorcycle tests, other than the John Rhodes Centre in Brampton.

The John Rhodes Centre uses the M.O.S.T. (Motorcycle Operator Skills Test). An explanation sheet for the M.O.S.T. is available at the Centre.

OBSERVATION POINT

START FINISH

Diagram 1-2

Motorcycle equipment requirements

(Under the Ontario Highway Traffic Act and regulations)

1) No person shall drive on or operate a motorcycle or motor assisted bicycle on a highway unless he is wearing a helmet that complies with the regulations and the chin strap of the helmet is securely fastened under the chin. [H.T.A. 104(1)]. Drivers are responsible for passengers under 16 years of age to ensure the passenger is wearing a helmet that complies with the regulations and the chin strap of the helmet is securely fastened under the chin. [H.T.A. 104 (2)]. All helmets must meet that standards of the Canadian Standards Association Standard D230, Snell Memorial Foundation, British Standards Institute, or United States of America Federal Motor Vehicle Safety Standard 218 and shall bear the symbol (DOT). All helmets must bear the appropriate monogram or certificate. [Reg. 610 (2)].

2) The lamp on the front of a motorcycle must cast a white light only, and the rear lamp, a red light. A white light must illuminate the registration plate. [H.T.A. 62 (2)] and [H.T.A. 62 (19)].

3) Every motorcycle must have two braking systems - one for the front wheel and one for the rear wheel - each with separate means of application. [H.T.A. 64 (2)].

4) Motorcycle handlebars must not be more than 380 mm (15 in.) in height above the uppermost portion of the seat provided for the operator when the seat is depressed by the weight of the operator. [Reg. 596-10 (1)].

5) You must not carry a passenger on your motorcycle unless the passenger is in a side car designed to carry a passenger or is sitting astride on a seat securely fastened behind the operator's seat and provided with foot rests. [Reg. 596-10 (2) (3)].

6) Motorcycles which have a cylinder swept volume of 50 cc or less, or those motorcycles driven by electricity are prohibited from most freeways. [Reg. 630].

7) For all motorcycles manufactured on or after January 1, 1970, lights must be illuminated at all times when on a highway [H.T.A. 62 (5)].

8) Every motor vehicle must be equipped with an alarm bell, gong or horn, which must be kept in good working condition. [H.T.A. 75 (5)].

9) A tire bearing,
   a) the words "not for highway use", "farm use only" or "competition circuit use only";
   b) the letters "SL", "NHS" or "TG" after the tire designation; or
   c) any other wording or lettering

indicating that the tire was not
designed for highway use, shall
not be installed on a motor
vehicle or trailer. [Reg. 625 s. 6].

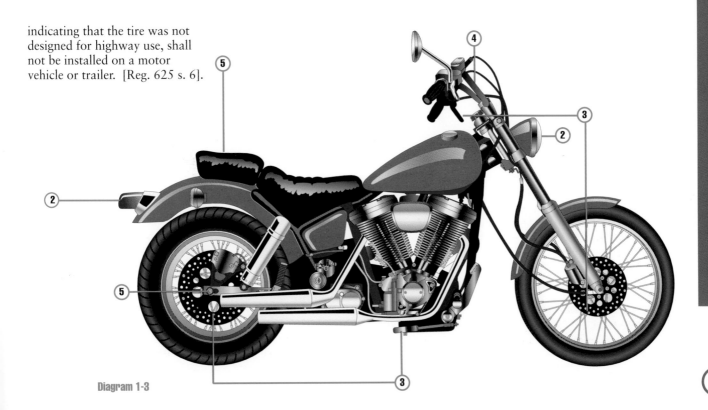

Diagram 1-3

Buying or selling a used vehicle

Safety standards certificate

When the ownership of a used motorcycle changes, a Safety Standards Certificate and proof of insurance by the new owner must be produced to the Ministry in order to change the registration record.

The required Safety Standards Certificate can only be obtained from a licensed Motor Vehicle Inspection Station authorized to inspect motorcycles.

Regulation 611 sets out the inspection procedures, inspection requirements and performance standards of the items to be inspected for a Safety Standards Certificate.

A certificate will not be issued for any motorcycle that fails to pass the prescribed inspection until the required repair or replacement is made.

A safety Standards Certificate outlines that the vehicle met inspection standards on the date certified. It is not a warranty or guarantee.

If you are selling a used vehicle privately in Ontario, you must buy a Used Vehicle Information Package. This applies to the private sale of any car, van, light truck, motor home or motorcycle. The package is available from any Ministry of Transportation Driver and Vehicle Licence Issuing Office or through the Ministry of Consumer and Commercial Relations.

The package, which the seller must show to potential buyers, has a description of the vehicle, its registration and lien history in Ontario, and the average wholesale and retail values for its model and year. It also includes information about retail sales tax.

As well as giving the buyer the Used Vehicle Information Package, sellers must remove their licence plates, sign the vehicle transfer portion of their vehicle permit and give it to the buyer. Sellers must keep the plate portion of the permit.

The buyer must take the package and the vehicle portion of the permit to a Driver and Vehicle Licence Issuing Office to register as the new owner within six days of the sale.

Before buyers can put their own plates on their new vehicle, they must have:

- their licence plates validated.
- the vehicle portion of the permit issued for the vehicle.
- their own licence plate number recorded on the plate portion of the vehicle permit.
- a valid Safety Standards Certificate.
- the minimum insurance required under the Compulsory Automobile Insurance Act.

Being in shape to drive your bike

Riding a motorcycle is more demanding than driving another vehicle. You must be in good physical and mental shape to drive safely. Three things that often keep motorcyclists from being in shape to drive safely are alcohol, drugs, and fatigue.

Alcohol

Alcohol impairment is a deadly trap – whether you're driving a motorcycle or driving any other vehicle. Drinking increases your chances of having a collision, whatever kind of vehicle you're driving. The difference is that a motorcyclist is far more likely to be killed or injured in the event of a collision. In 1993, alcohol was involved in 40 percent of all fatal motorcycle collisions in Ontario.

Alcohol can begin to affect your ability to handle your motorcycle safely at blood-alcohol levels far below the legal limit. Your balance, steering, speed control and distance perception may be off – and because alcohol also clouds your judgement, you may not recognize these symptoms of impairment until it's too late.

It's an offence under the Criminal Code of Canada to drive your motorcycle when your ability is impaired by alcohol or drugs, or when your blood-alcohol concentration is more than 0.08 percent. If you're stopped by the police before you have a collision, you could be liable on conviction to a fine or prison term, and your driver's licence could be suspended for a year or more.

If you aren't stopped, and you kill or injure someone other than yourself, the penalties on conviction are far more severe – up to 14 years in prison and, once you get out, up to ten years prohibition from driving any kind of vehicle. In very serious cases, you could be charged with manslaughter or criminal negligence, and face the possibility of life imprisonment and a lifetime prohibition from driving.

You can lose a lot more than your licence drinking and driving.

Ministry of the Attorney General

Being in shape to drive your bike

Other drugs

Almost any drug can affect the skills that you need to drive a motorcycle safely. This includes prescription drugs as well as illegal drugs. It even includes such everyday drugs as cold tablets or allergy pills. Such drugs can leave you weak, dizzy, or drowsy. Make sure you know the effects of any drug before you attempt to drive. If you feel dizzy or weak while you're riding, stop and wait until you feel normal.

Remember – the Criminal Code definition of impaired includes drugs as well as alcohol.

Fatigue

Fatigue impairs your ability to perceive and react to emergencies.

Here are some things you can do to prevent fatigue:

1. Protect yourself from the elements. Wind, cold, and rain make you tire quickly. Dress warmly. A fairing or windshield is worth its cost, if you plan to do a lot of travelling.
2. Limit your distance.
3. Take frequent rest breaks. Stop and get off the bike.

If you ever feel that you don't want to drive your bike – then DON'T. If you're overly excited or depressed, leave the bike at home, because that's the day you may be in a collision.

Remember...riding a bike takes your full concentration and attention!

PREPARING TO DRIVE

Drivers' chances of getting to their destination safely are affected by things done before starting out.

Good drivers always begin a trip with:

1. Proper helmet.
2. A check of the motorcycle.
3. Protective clothing.

The helmet

An approved motorcycle helmet can protect you from serious head injury. When a motorcycle falls, the driver's head often hits something hard, the pavement, curb, etc.

The human head is fragile and head injuries are often fatal or crippling. It is the law in Ontario that drivers and passengers must wear approved helmets and have them properly fastened. A surprising number of motorcyclists killed in collisions were not wearing their helmets. Wear your helmet every time you drive.

Preparing to drive

Proper helmet

A poor helmet is little better than no helmet.

A helmet must:

1. Meet standards approved for use in Ontario (see page 10)
2. Have a strong chin strap and fastener.
3. Be free of defects such as cracks, loose padding, frayed straps, or exposed metal.

It's a good idea to have a helmet that is a bright colour such as red, white, yellow or orange. It should also have reflective material on the back and the sides. However, check the helmet manufacturer's instructions before using any adhesive on your helmet.

When selecting a helmet, make sure that it is properly fitted to your head. When you put it on, make sure it is snug and the strap is securely fastened. Studies of motorcycle crashes show that a loose helmet is not effective at all, because it will come off in a collision. In general, full faced helmets offer the best protection.

Eye and face protection

Your eyes need protection from wind, dust, rain, insects, small pebbles thrown up from other vehicles and other debris. A face shield is best, it protects your whole face.

Eyeglasses are not made to protect drivers. They will shatter if hit by a flying object. If you wear glasses, also use a face shield.

To be effective, eye or face protection must:

1. Be free of scratches.
2. Be made of material that doesn't shatter.
3. Give a clear view to either side.
4. Fasten securely so that it can't be blown off.
5. Allow some air to pass through so it won't fog.
6. Allow enough room for eyeglasses or sunglasses, if needed.

Tinted goggles or face shields should not be worn at night.

Protective clothing

Clothing is not just for comfort, but protection. It can help protect you from injury in case of a fall and will help reduce fatigue by keeping you comfortable regardless of the weather. Bright colours and reflective items, such as a safety vest, make you more visible.

Jacket and pants should cover your arms and legs completely. Wear a jacket even in warm weather. Leather is the best. However, nylon, vinyl and other sturdy synthetic materials can give you a lot of protection. But they have been known to melt and stick to the skin when skidding on grass or pavement. Your clothes should fit snugly enough to keep from flapping and yet let you move freely. You should consider protective equipment such as "back protectors" and body "armour" inserts in your protective clothing.

In cold or wet weather, your clothes should keep you warm and dry as well as protect you against injury. You can't control a motorcycle well if you are numb. Riding for long periods in cold weather can cause severe chill and fatigue. A winter jacket should resist wind and fit snugly at the neck, wrists, and waist. Rain suits should be one-piece. Those that are not designed for motorcycle use may balloon and allow wind and water to enter at highway speeds.

Boots or shoes should be sturdy and high enough to protect the ankles. Soles should be made of hard, durable material. Heels should be short so they don't catch on rough surfaces. Don't wear shoes with rings or loose laces that may catch on controls.

Gloves are also important. They give you a better hold on the hand-grips and controls. Gauntlet gloves are recommended. They provide protection to not only fingers and knuckles, but wrists as well in case of a collision.

Diagram 2-1

Know your motorcycle controls

The beauty of motorcycle design is that all controls and other important devices are within quick reach of the driver's hands and feet. Twenty controls and devices, for example, are displayed in this illustration.

1. Speedometer & Odometer
2. Tripmeter
3. Tachometer
4. Ignition Switch
5. Light Switches
6. Turn Signal Switch
7. Horn Button
8. Fuel Supply Valve
9. Choke Control
10. Throttle
11. Clutch Lever
12. Gear Selector
13. Front Brake Lever
14. Rear Brake Pedal
15. Starter
16. Engine Kill Switch
17. Stands
18. Oil Pressure Warning Light
19. Rear View Mirrors
20. Fuel Gauge

It is important to become familiar with the motorcycle's controls, whether you're learning to drive or are an experienced driver driving an unfamiliar motorcycle.

The same control may not be found in the same place on all motorcycles. Check your owner's manual for the exact location and precise method of operation of all controls and devices. The first step in learning to drive a motorcycle is to learn the controls used to operate the machine. You must be able to reach any control without looking for it. You don't want to take your eyes off the road to find your controls, because traffic patterns and road conditions can change quickly. With practice, you will be able to operate all controls by reflex. Automatic response is required before you can venture out into traffic.

Diagram 2-2

Instruments

The following instruments are grouped in the centre of the handlebars on most motorcycles:

- **Speedometer** indicates riding speed in kilometres per hour or miles per hour.
- **Odometer** indicates total kilometres or miles accumulated on the motorcycle.
- **Tripmeter** indicates kilometres or miles accumulated since the last time it was re-set at zero.
- **Tachometer** indicates engine speed in revolutions per minute (RPM) and shows with a red line the maximum RPM the engine can safely attain.
- **High beam indicator light** shows in red or blue when the headlight is on high beam.
- **Neutral indicator light** shows green when the transmission is in neutral.
- **Turn signal indicator light** flashes amber when either left or right signals are operating.

Know your motorcycle controls

Ignition switch

The ignition key goes into the ignition switch located near the centre of the handlebars or below one side of the fuel tank. On and Off positions are standard. Some switches also have LIGHTS and PARK positions. When the ignition is on, the engine can be started in either the ON or LIGHTS position. The LIGHTS position turns on the headlight and the taillight. The PARK position turns on only the taillight. The key can be removed only in the OFF, PARK and LOCK positions.

Light switches

If the ignition switch does not have a LIGHTS position, your motorcycle will have a separate switch with which to turn on the headlights and taillight. On all recent motorcycles, the headlight and taillight will come on automatically when the ignition is switched ON and the engine is running.

A dimmer switch generally located on the left handlebar and operated by the left thumb can be used to set the headlight on low or high beam.

Turn-signal switch

The switch to control turn signals is usually located on the left handlebar and is actuated with the left thumb. The switch is moved right to R to flash the right signal lights, front and rear. It is moved left to L to flash the left signal lights.

Most motorcycle turn signals do not self-cancel after a turn, as an automobile's do. So, you must cancel the signal after each turn or lane change. Failure to cancel a turn signal is as dangerous as not signalling in the first place, because it may cause other drivers to pull out or turn in front of you. If your motorcycle has no self cancelling turn signals make sure you turn them off or reset the signal when appropriate.

Brake light

The brake light is located on the rear fender and on newer motorcycles is activated when either the front or rear brake is applied.

Horn button

The horn can be sounded by pushing with the left thumb the horn button located on the left handlebar.

Fuel supply valve

The fuel-supply valve is a petcock located below the fuel tank and controls the flow of gasoline to the engine. When the motorcycle is not in use, the valve should always be turned to the OFF position to eliminate the possibility of fuel leaking into the crankcase or creating a fire hazard.

The valve must be turned to the ON position on many bikes for fuel to flow to the engine. The fuel tank has a reserve section in case the main section runs dry. To release the reserve supply, you must turn the valve to RESERVE or RES, something which you should be able to do while your motorcycle is in motion. You should have an idea of how far your bike will travel on a tank of gas and be able to recognize the stumble or hesitation caused by an almost empty tank.

Choke control

The choke adjusts the mixture of gasoline and air supplied to the engine and usually is used only when starting a cold engine. The choke control is located on the engine or at the handlebars. To start a cold engine, move the choke control to the ON position and start the motorcycle. When the engine is warm, return the choke control to the OFF position.

Know your motorcycle controls

Throttle
The right handlebar grip is the throttle that controls the flow of fuel to the engine and thus the speed of the engine and ultimately the speed of the motorcycle. To increase speed, rotate the throttle toward you with your right hand. To reduce speed, twist the throttle away from you. The throttle should spring back to the idle position if you remove your hand.

Clutch lever
The clutch lever is located in front of the left handlebar and is operated when squeezed toward the handle grip with the fingers of the left hand. Squeezing the lever disengages the clutch and disconnects the engine power from the rear wheel. Releasing the lever engages the clutch and provides power to the rear wheel. Whenever you change gears, either up or down, you must first disengage the clutch.

Gear-shift
The gear-selector is located on the left side of most motorcycles just ahead of the footrest.

Most motorcycles have five or six gears and a neutral position. In neutral, the transmission is out of gear and power will not reach the rear wheel.

On the majority of bikes, neutral is located between first and second gear. Always start and shut off your bike in neutral.

The gear-selector should only be operated while the clutch is disengaged. After you have squeezed the clutch lever with your left hand, you can select the gear you need by lifting or depressing the gear-selector with the toe of your left boot.

Front-brake lever

The front-wheel brake is applied by squeezing the lever on the right handle-bar toward the handgrip with your right hand.

Rear-brake pedal

The rear-wheel brake is activated when pressure is applied by your right foot on the pedal located in front of the right footrest (on most bikes). Remember that the right hand controls the front brake while the right foot controls the rear brake. They are used together. The engine on your motor-cycle will also act as a brake when you gear down or reduce throttle.

Starters

Most motorcycles have electric starters operated by pushing the starter button on the right handlebar.

Many bikes have a kick starter, usually located above the right footrest. It must be unfolded before it can be used to start the motorcycle with a vigorous kick.

Engine-kill switch

The engine-kill switch is located on the right han-dlebar and is usual-ly red in colour. It is used in an emergency to stop the engine quickly. It may also be used to turn off the engine after a normal stop, but be sure to turn off the igni-tion switch as well after using the kill switch.

The engine **will not start** when the kill switch is in the OFF position.

Stands

When motorcycles are parked, they are supported by either side stands or centre stands. Larger models have both.

A side stand extends downward from its position underneath the motorcycle to support the motorcy-cle in a leaned position.

The centre stand is attached under-neath the centre of the motorcycle frame and is capable of supporting the motorcycle in a vertical position.

Stands are held in their retracted positions by spring mechanisms and lowered for use by the driver's foot.

Make sure your side stand is retracted before riding off.

Daily motorcycle check

With a little experience, you will become familiar with the motorcycle controls. Furthermore, if there's anything wrong with the motorcycle, the time to find out about it is before you are in the middle of traffic. Here are the things you should check before every drive. Take a look at the critical parts of your bike before starting out.

Tires

Since you only have two tires, keep them in good condition. Check for:

Inflation
The motorcycle does not handle properly if the air pressure is too low or too high. Check the owner's manual for the right amount of air.

Tread
Worn or uneven tread can make the motorcycle skid, particularly on wet pavement.

Damage
Check for cuts or nails stuck in the tread. Also, the sidewalls should be checked for cracks. A blowout on a motorcycle can be extremely dangerous.

Controls

The controls are mounted on the handlebars. The steering is done in conjunction with your body by leaning. Make sure your controls are in working order before you start out.

Brakes

Try the front and rear brakes one at a time. Make sure each one holds the motorcycle when it is fully applied.

Clutch and throttle

Make sure the controls work smoothly. The throttle should snap closed when you let go.

Cables

Check the cables for kinks or broken strands. If a cable breaks while you are riding, a collision could result.

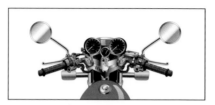

Lights

Don't put your faith in lights that may not work. Keep them clean and check them regularly.

Turn signals

Check all four turn signal lights. Make sure they flash when they are turned on and are bright enough to be seen.

Headlight

Check your headlight. In day time, pass your hand in front of the beam to make sure the headlight is really on. At night, try your dimmer switch to make sure both high and low beams are working.

Tail and brake light

Try each of your brake controls and make sure that each one activates your brake light.

Daily motorcycle check

Accessories

Horn
Try the horn. The time to find out it doesn't work is long before someone fails to see you.

Mirrors
Clean and adjust both your mirrors before you start. It is difficult and dangerous to drive with one hand while you try to adjust a mirror.

Swing your mirrors outward far enough to see around your own body. Adjust each mirror so that it lets you see about half of the lane behind you and as much as possible of the lane next to you.

Reduce your blind spot to the minimum. Don't forget that mirrors are not a substitute for shoulder checks.

Fluids

Gas
Check gas and oil levels before you start. Be sure you have enough. Running out of gas is certainly frustrating, and can be dangerous if it happens where you cannot get off the road safely. Be sure you can switch to your reserve tank (RES) easily without fumbling. Use your tripmeter as a fuel consumption gauge.

Oil
Check your oil level before starting. Engine damage can result from oil that is too low or dirty. Your oil level can be checked through the oil level window or on your dip stick.

Lack of oil can cause your engine to "seize". In addition to damaging your engine, this could lock the rear wheel and cause you to lose control.

PRECISION – LEARNING TO CONTROL A MOTORCYCLE LIKE AN EXPERT

To control a motorcycle with precision, you have to be able to make it go exactly where you want and at the right speed.

When you're learning to drive, it's important to develop proper riding techniques, right from the start. However, only a lot of practice will ensure that you are able to control steering, throttle and brakes precisely.

You should first check that the motorcycle isn't too heavy or large for you to operate it comfortably. When sitting on the seat, you should be able to place your feet flat on the ground.

Body position

To control a motorcycle well, your body must be in the proper position.

Posture

Your body should be fairly erect. This lets you use your arms to steer the motorcycle rather than to hold yourself up.

Sit close enough to the handlebars to reach them with your arms slightly bent. Bending your arms allows you to turn the handlebars without having to stretch.

Precision – learning to control a motorcycle like an expert

Hands

Hold the handgrips firmly, so that you will not lose your grip if the motorcycle bounces. Drive with your wrists low. This "broken-wrist" position will help prevent unintended acceleration.

Knees

Hold your knees firmly against the gas tank for comfort and better control. This will help you keep your balance as the motorcycle turns.

Feet

Keep your feet firmly on the foot rests. A firm footing is important to help you maintain balance. Don't drag your foot along the ground. If your foot catches on something, you could lose control of the motorcycle.

Keep your feet near the controls. This lets you use the controls quickly if you have to. Also, try to keep your toes up. If you let them drop down, they may get caught between the road surface and the footrest.

Turning

New drivers tend to have more trouble turning than experienced drivers. The only way to learn how to make good, precise turns is to practice. Here are two important tips for practising.

1-Limit your speed

Slow down on a turn. Don't take turns too fast. Approach turns extra carefully until you learn to judge how fast you can actually take a turn. If you can't hold a turn, you may end up crossing into another lane of traffic or going off the road. If you brake too hard when turning, you may skid out of control.

Remember, it is much better to enter a turn too slow than too fast. It is better to speed up as you come out of a turn than to slow down, or brake drastically while you're in the turn.

Diagram 3-1

2-Lean with the motorcycle

Both you and the motorcycle lean into a turn together. The sharper the turn and the faster your speed, the more you lean. Look well ahead in your turn. Practice keeping your head upright and facing into the turn.

Braking

Your motorcycle has two brakes. You need both of them to stop effectively. The front brake is the more important of the two brakes. It provides about three-quarters of your stopping power.

Here are some tips for effective braking:

1. Use all fingers to pull in the front brake lever smoothly.
2. Get into the habit of using both brakes everytime you slow down or stop. If you use only the rear brake for "normal" stops, you may not have enough skill to use the front brake properly when you really need it.
3. Apply both brakes at the same time.
4. Until you learn the cornering limits of your motorcycle, be especially careful to slow down enough for turns. Do all your braking before you get into your turn, if you can.

5. You can use both brakes in a turn. Some people wrongly think using the front brake in a turn is dangerous. It is no more dangerous to use both brakes in a turn than it is when you are stopping in a straight line. However, the motorcycle will fall down if the front brake is used so hard that it locks the wheel. As you gain more experience, you will learn how to brake in a turn smoothly and safely.

Shifting gears

There is more to shifting gears than simply getting the motorcycle to accelerate smoothly. Sloppy shifting can cause collisions when down shifting, turning, or starting on hills.

The purpose of the gears in a motorcycle transmission is to match the engine's speed (measured by the tachometer in rpm) with the motorcycle's road speed (measured by the speedometer).

Precision – learning to control a motorcycle like an expert

As you accelerate, the transmission must be shifted up through the gears to maintain the motorcycle's road speed without the engine turning too fast. Your motorcycle owner's manual has information on the range of engine speeds at which the motorcycle was designed to be operated.

When slowing down in traffic, or for road conditions, you must shift down through the gears until an appropriate match is obtained between engine and road speed. The proper gear will also permit the engine to provide sufficient power for the bike to accelerate if necessary. Remember you **shift up** when the engine is turning **too fast** for the road speed and you **shift down** when the engine is turning **too slowly**.

Shifting down is more difficult to do smoothly than shifting up. You must open the throttle slightly, to increase engine speed, as you shift down with the clutch pulled in. If you don't apply enough throttle, the bike will lurch when you release the clutch. Shifting down without having the engine speed up enough to match its speed with the motorcycle's speed may cause the rear wheel to skid.

Shifting in a turn

Do not up shift or down shift in a turn. A rough, jerky down shift can cause the rear wheel to lock resulting in a skid. Applying too much power in a turn can cause the rear tire to lose traction, also resulting in a skid. It is best to change gears before entering a turn.

Starting on a hill

It is more difficult to get your motorcycle moving off smoothly on an upgrade than it is on level ground. There is a greater possibility you will stall or roll backward.

Here is what you have to do:

1. Use the front brake to hold the motorcycle while you start the engine and shift into first gear.
2. Change to the foot brake to hold the cycle while you operate the throttle with your right hand.
3. Open the throttle a little bit for more power.
4. Release the clutch gradually. If you release it too quickly, the front wheel may come off the ground or the engine may stall – or both.
5. Release the foot brake when the clutch begins to take hold.

BEING AWARE AND ALERT
Seeing like an expert, thinking like an expert

Driving a motorcycle well is tough. Once you have mastered the basics of the machine, the next step is to learn how to handle it on the road. Road skills take time and practice to learn. The novice driver's most important asset is **awareness**. What is awareness? Giving full attention to what you're **seeing** and **hearing**, then judging what is happening around you. Your eyes, ears and other senses must keep you safe and out of trouble.

An alert driver can decide what to expect and what is going to happen next. As you drive along, you have to see and understand what is happening around you so that you can be in the right place and travelling at the right speed to avoid surprises.

Traffic situations can be complicated. You often have to see and understand many things very quickly in order to be aware of what will happen next. For instance, you may have to decide what other drivers at an intersection are going to do. This is why you have to learn good road skills.

The best way to avoid trouble is to see it coming. Because they see and understand possible problems before getting to them, expert drivers have very few surprises on the road.

Skilled drivers have learned to look far ahead. In the city, they look from one half to one full block ahead. On the highway, they look as far ahead as they can see. Looking well ahead gives plenty of time to adjust to problems. It also helps to avoid panic stops or sudden swerves that can cause even more trouble.

Being aware and alert

To develop expert driver awareness:

1. Look ahead as far as you can see.

2. Keep your **eyes moving**. Don't look at one place for more than two seconds; trouble could be developing in one place while you're staring at another.

3. Use your height advantage. Look over or through the car in front of you for cars stopping or turning ahead.

4. Check the roadside. Watch for cars that may leave the curb or enter from side streets or driveways.

Sometimes you cannot see an area because your view is blocked by a bridge or a truck. Good drivers have good imagination. Ask yourself what **might** be there that you can't see yet. What you can't see **can** hurt you.

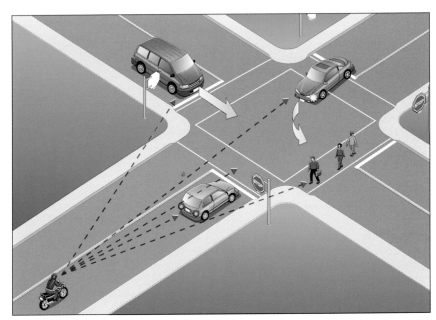

Diagram 4-1

Checking the Road Surface

Road conditions and surfaces cause more trouble for motorcycles than other vehicles. When looking ahead and scanning the road, good drivers always look for problem spots on the surface. They learn to see these spots **well ahead**, so they don't have too look down at the road surface.

1. Keep checking the road surface ahead for slippery spots, bad bumps, broken pavement, loose gravel, metal plates, polished pavement, wet leaves, or objects lying in the road.
2. When riding in winter conditions be alert for ice or snow patches on the road.

Using Mirrors

Traffic behind is almost as important to the motorcycle driver as traffic ahead. Good drivers check their mirrors every few seconds. Frequent mirror checks will help you keep track of traffic coming up behind you. You should have a good picture in your mind of what is back there, so you won't be caught off guard if somebody passes you. You also want to know so you can stop quickly or swerve if any emergency develops up front.

Mirror checks are important in certain situations:
1. When you have to slow down or stop suddenly. There may be someone close behind you.
2. When you are stopped at an intersection. Check cars approaching from behind.

In both of these situations, if the driver behind you isn't paying attention, they could be right on top of you before they notice you are there. You have to be prepared to take evasive action to get out of the way.
3. Anytime you turn. Check cars behind, especially if you plan to slow down and turn where others may not expect it, such as alleys, driveways, and side streets.

Again the driver behind you may not see you or slow down. It may be better not to turn but continue on.
4. Anytime you change lanes. Make sure no one is about to pass you.

Many motorcycles have rounded "convex" mirrors. They give a wider view of the road behind them than flat mirrors do. However, they also make cars seem farther away than they really are. If you are not used to convex mirrors, try this: While you are stopped, pick out a parked car in your mirror. Try to form a mental image of how far away it is. Then turn around and look at it. See how close you came. Practice this until you become a good judge of distance. Even then, allow extra distance before you change lanes.

Being aware and alert

Remember, mirrors don't give you the whole traffic picture, so **always make a final shoulder check**, by turning your head, before you turn or change lanes.

Learning to Anticipate

The traffic laws and rules of driving courtesy tell what drivers are **supposed** to do in any given situation.

Good drivers are always asking themselves what other drivers are **really** going to do, not what they are **supposed** to do.

In order to anticipate what another road user may do, the driver has to think about two different things:

1. What does the other driver want to do? Put yourself in the driver's seat. See yourself and other vehicles on the road as he or she may see the situation.

2. Does the other driver see me?

The other drivers on the road basically want to get where they're going without delay. They will do whatever they have to do to keep moving. For instance, if a driver's lane is blocked by a stalled car, the motorist will want to change lanes to keep moving. If the driver is stopped at a stop sign, he or she will want to pull out as soon as possible.

The next question is: **Do they see me?**

You can't assume other drivers have seen you. Drivers of other vehicles that have collided with motorcyclists often say they didn't see the motorcycle until it was too late.

A motorcycle is more difficult to see than other vehicles. Your profile is smaller from most angles. Even if you are seen, you are in danger of having your speed or distance from other vehicles misjudged.

If a driver does not see you, he or she will pull out, or turn in front of you, or cut you off. **Even if the driver does see you, you might be hit if they:**

1. misjudge your speed,

2. are drunk or impaired or

3. are just careless of your well being.

Headlight

In Ontario, the headlight and tail-light on most modern motorcycles must be turned on all the time, even in the daytime. This improves the chances of the motorcycle being seen by other drivers.

The headlight helps a lot, but it's not the whole solution to the motorcycle visibility problem during the day. The headlight is most visible from straight ahead of the motorcycle. From an angle it doesn't look very bright and can't help much. From the side and rear, of course, it has no effect at all. Taillights aren't bright enough to help much during the day either.

Diagram 4-2

Only the motorcycle driver can make the motorcycle more noticeable. There are a number of things you can do to be more visible in addition to keeping your headlight on.

Clothing

Wear bright colours. They help to make you visible. Bright coloured clothing and helmet will help the motorcyclist be more visible during the day, especially from the angles where the headlight can't help. Yellow, orange, red and other bright colours are highly visible. Black and dark colours are not. Think about wearing a reflective vest, especially at night. Consider adding reflective tape to your helmet, clothing and motorcycle. In the rain, wear a reflective rainsuit.

Nighttime visibility

At night you depend mostly on your lights to be sure other drivers see you. This works pretty well most of the time, but not always. If you're riding alone on a dark road, your headlight will be very visible to a driver ahead. But if you're in traffic with other headlights behind you, a driver ahead may not be able to pick your single light out of all the lights behind. This problem is especially bad when the roads are wet, because of the lights reflecting off the road surface.

If you're ahead of a group of cars at night, slow down. Other drivers are even more likely than usual to turn in front of you.

Nighttime visibility to sides and rear is helped by the taillight and side reflectors. Again, the single taillight can get lost against the background of other lights. And it can be hard for drivers to tell how far away the light is, even if they see it. You can help by adding reflectors or reflective tape to the rear of the bike.

Keep your foot on the brake, day or night, when stopped for a stop sign or traffic signal.

Being aware and alert

Lane position

Think about your lane position. Sometimes you can make yourself more visible by moving side to side in a lane, or changing lanes where appropriate.

Horn

The horn on most motorcycles is not much of an attention getter. Nevertheless, be ready to use it whenever you're passing a car, or approaching a driveway or intersection with a vehicle in it that might pull out in front of you. Also, it's a good idea to use your horn before you pass anyone you think might move into your lane.

Here are some situations to watch for:

1. A driver is in the lane next to you and coming up behind a vehicle ahead.
2. A parked car that has someone in it.
3. Someone is walking or riding a bicycle in the street.

Don't be afraid to **use your horn** if you have any doubts about what others might do.

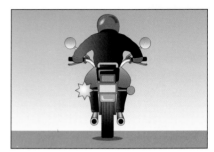

Diagram 4-3

Signalling

Turn signals do two things for you. First, they tell others what you plan to do. Use them anytime you change lanes whether someone else is around or not. Remember, it's when you don't see the other vehicle that your signals are most important.

Second, your signal lights make you more visible. A driver behind you is more likely to see your turn signal than your taillight. Therefore, **make it a habit to use your turn signals** even when what you plan to do is obvious. For example, if you use your turn signals on a freeway entrance ramp, it's more likely that cars on the freeway will see you and make room for you.

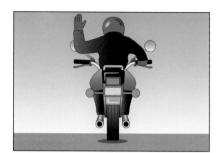

Caution

Diagram 4-4

Forgetting to turn a signal off is as dangerous as forgetting to turn it on. A driver may think you plan to turn and pull into your path. Check your instrument panel to see if you've left a signal on.

If you have an old motorcycle without turn signals, use the standard hand signals. (See The Official Driver's Handbook.)

Brake light

Diagram 4-5

You can help others notice you by tapping the brake pedal lightly to flash your brake light before you slow down. It's important to flash your brake light as a signal that you're going to slow down when:
1. You're being closely followed.
2. You're making a tight turn off a high-speed highway.
3. You're slowing or turning in the middle of a block, at an alley, or at some place where others might not expect you to turn.

Eye contact

Diagram 4-6

Try to make eye contact with other drivers to let them know you see them. Shoulder check often to make sure other drivers aren't crowding you.

Being aware and alert

Left turn in front of motorcycle

One of the most common causes of motorcycle/car collisions is the car driver turning left in front of the motorcycle. The car driver either doesn't see the motorcycle or misjudges its speed. The motorcycle driver may not be completely innocent in this situation. If your motorcycle is going faster than a driver would expect when you approach an intersection with a car waiting to turn left:

1. Prepare to slow down and proceed with caution.
2. Take a defensive lane position. Move as far as possible to the right to give a little more room between yourself and the car.
3. Think about what you'll do if the car turns in front of you. Where will you go? Is there a clear area to swerve? How fast will your bike stop on that pavement surface?

Diagram 4-7

4. Don't let your mind focus too long on the left turning vehicle. Is there something else in the intersection that could cause trouble too? Another car, a pedestrian?

POSITION Learning Your Place on the Road

Motorcyclists don't have the protection around them that other drivers have. So they have to make their own protection.

Lane position – blocking

A motorcycle driver has some choice of where to drive in the lane. The best choice is the "blocking position", a little to one side of the centre of the lane. The blocking position discourages other drivers from trying to squeeze past in the same lane as the motorcycle.

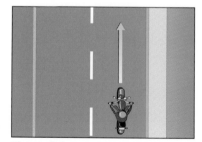

Diagram 5-1

Position 1 Wrong

The centre of the lane does not provide a "blocking position". It is coated with oil thrown from cars and is slippery when wet.

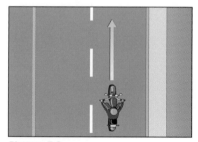

Diagram 5-2

Position 2 Correct
When travelling in the CURB LANE

A motorcycle driver, when travelling in the right lane should be slightly to the left of the centre of the lane. This is your "blocking position" for the right lane of a two-lane road.

Learning your place on the road

Diagram 5-3

Diagram 5-4

Position 3
When travelling in the PASSING LANE

By travelling in this position – just slightly to the right of the centre of the lane, you're in a "blocking position" – the proper riding position in this lane.

Position 4
CENTRE or "TRANSIT" LANE

When riding on a freeway with three or more lanes, avoid travelling in the centre lane, if possible, because you don't have a "blocking position".

Position for turning

Good drivers are careful to maintain the proper "blocking position" when they make turns.

Position 5
Making a proper RIGHT TURN (No change in lane size at intersection)

When approaching an intersection where the curb lane remains the same size, stay in the normal "blocking position"; make your turn and move to the proper lane position after completing the turn.
(Diagram 5-5)

Position 5A
Making a proper RIGHT TURN (when lane opens up at intersection)

It's more complicated, when approaching an intersection where the lane opens up. Because the stop line is further out, you must move over from your normal "blocking position" in the curb lane to prevent a car from coming up on the inside on the wider part of the road. Make a shoulder check; move over to the right of the centre of the lane; make your right turn and than make another shoulder check and move back to the proper "blocking position" – to the left of the centre of the lane. (Diagram 5-6)

Diagram 5-5

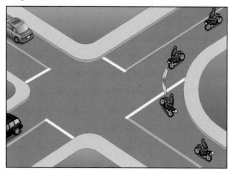
Diagram 5-6

Learning your place on the road

Position 6
Making a proper LEFT TURN (from curb lane to curb lane)
In the curb lane, you make your turn keeping the "blocking position" throughout your turn. This is the position when making your turn from a two-lane street or highway to a two-lane street or highway.

Position 6A
Making a proper LEFT TURN (from passing lane to passing lane)
Motorcyclist stays in the proper "blocking position" throughout the turn – just right of the centre of the lane.

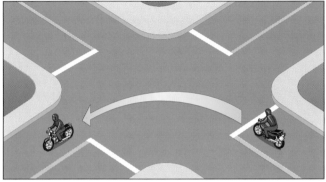

Diagram 5-7

Diagram 5-8

The best protection a driver can have is distance – distance between the driver and other people's mistakes.

1. Time to react to trouble.
2. Some place to go.

You should maintain a "circle of safety" around you and keep your defensive eye alert for all other traffic:

The vehicles in front of you; behind you; approaching you; approaching from the side; the vehicles you are passing and; any vehicle passing you.

Diagram 5-9: **Circle of Safety**

Learning your place on the road

Distance in front

Good drivers keep at least two seconds distance between themselves and the vehicle ahead. This gives them plenty of time to react if something happens up ahead. It also gives a better view of things in the road, such as potholes, slippery spots, chunks of tire tread, or debris. If conditions are less than ideal, such as in bad weather, even greater following distances should be used.

For proper following distance, use the two second rule:

A. The car ahead is approaching a check point (a hydro pole, road sign, etc.)

B. Begin counting as the rear of the car ahead passes the check point.

C. Two seconds (one-thousand-one, one-thousand-two) is correct for ideal conditions.

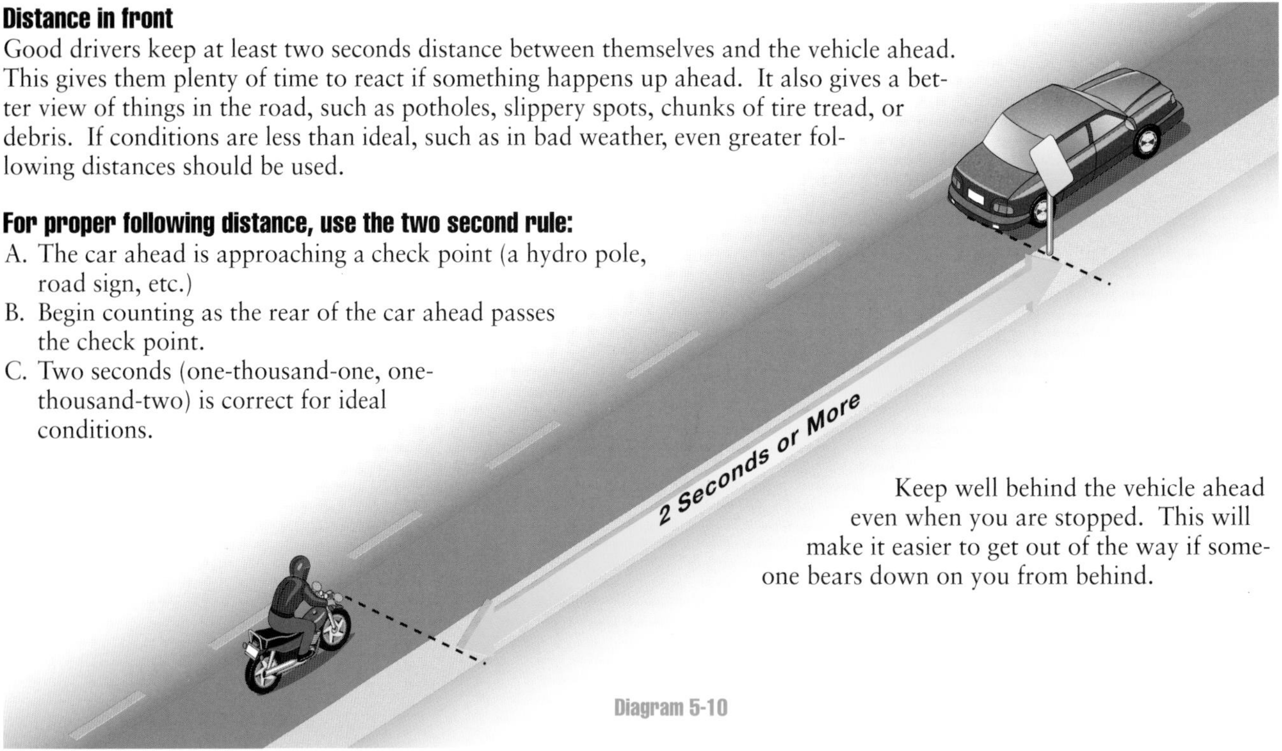

2 Seconds or More

Keep well behind the vehicle ahead even when you are stopped. This will make it easier to get out of the way if someone bears down on you from behind.

Diagram 5-10

Distance to the side

Motorcycle drivers can do one thing other drivers cannot – they can move across the lane to increase their distance from other vehicles. An experienced driver changes position in the lane as traffic conditions change.

Vehicles alongside

Don't drive alongside other vehicles if there is no need. A vehicle in the next lane could change into your lane at any time without warning. Vehicles in the next lane also block your escape if you run into danger in your lane. Speed up or drop back until you find a place that is clear on both sides.

Here are some of the conditions that require changes in lane position:

Passing vehicles

When you're being passed by an oncoming vehicle, or from behind, move a little toward the centre of the lane. There's no point in being any closer to a passing vehicle than you have to be. A slight mistake by

either driver could cause a side swipe. Moving towards the centre of the lane also helps to keep you out of the way of extended mirrors or things thrown from windows.

Give way to large trucks. They can create air turbulence that affects your control. You have more room for error if you move over, away from the truck.

Diagram 5-11

Learning your place on the road

Diagram 5-12

Parked cars

When passing parked cars, the motorcycle driver has an advantage over the automobile driver. By staying in the left portion of the lane, you can avoid the problems caused by doors opening, drivers getting out of cars, or people stepping from between cars.

A bigger problem is cars pulling out. Drivers often take a quick look behind them and fail to see a motorcycle. Cars making U-turns are a particular danger. The motorcyclist sees them pull out and slows down or changes lanes to let them enter. Then suddenly the car turns across the road and blocks the lane. This leaves the motorcyclist with no place to go. If you see a car pulling out, approach very cautiously.

Watch those lane changes

Weaving in and out of heavy traffic is a sure sign of an inexperienced or careless driver, and is dangerous. When you are travelling in heavy traffic stay in the same lane as much as possible.

When you have to change lanes, make sure there's no overtaking traffic by checking your mirrors. If it is safe, signal and look again in your mirror and then turn your head and make a shoulder check before changing lanes.

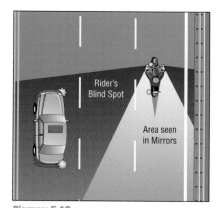

Diagram 5-13

Turn your head and make a shoulder check.

That's the only sure way to see a vehicle behind you in the next lane. It's particularly important. There's very little chance a driver in the next lane can react quickly enough to avoid you once you've started to move.

On a roadway with several lanes, check the far lanes as well as the one next to you. Another driver may be headed for the same space you are.

Lane sharing

Cars and motorcycles each need a full lane in which to operate safety. Motorcycle drivers shouldn't share lanes with cars. The best way to stop lane sharing is to keep your "blocking position" especially in situations where other drivers might be tempted to squeeze by you.

Such situations include:

1. Heavy bumper to bumper traffic.
2. When you're preparing to turn at an intersection, enter an exit lane, or leave the highway.
3. When another driver wants to pass you.

If you move to the far side of the lane in these situations, you invite the driver to share the lane with you.

Diagram 5-14

Learning your place on the road

Lane splitting

Don't do it! In heavy traffic, some drivers try "lane splitting", riding on the line between lanes of traffic. **This is extremely dangerous for the driver.** It puts the bike too close to other vehicles, and other drivers aren't expecting the motorcycle to be there. Just a small movement, a car starting a lane change or a door opening can cause an unavoidable crash. There's just no place to go.

Aside from the danger to the driver who does it, lane splitting causes trouble for all motorcycle drivers. It breaks down the respect other motorists should have for motorcyclists and tells them that drivers think it's alright to share lanes.

Diagram 5-15

Distance behind

Many drivers complain about "tailgaters", that is, people who follow others very closely. If someone is following you too closely, change lanes and let the tailgater pass.

If a driver still follows you too closely:

1. Increase your following distance from the vehicle ahead. This gives you and the tailgater more time to react in an emergency.
2. When the way is clear for a safe pass, slow down so the tailgater can pass.

Shoulder driving

Driving off the travelled portion of the roadway and onto the right shoulder is not permitted, unless the shoulder is paved and you are passing a vehicle that is making a left turn.

Passing on the left shoulder, paved or not, is prohibited.

Position for seeing

As a motorcycle driver, you can put yourself in a position to see things that another driver cannot see.

Blind curves

You move to one side of the lane or the other to get a better view through the curve.

Diagram 5-16

Diagram 5-17

Learning your place on the road

At blind intersections

After stopping, you can ease forward past obstructions to see properly if anyone is coming.

At the roadside

You can angle a motorcycle across the road so that you can see both directions.

Diagram 5-18

Diagram 5-19

Position for being seen

Where the driver positions the motorcycle on the road also affects how well other drivers can see it. Experienced drivers think about what other drivers can see from where they are. These drivers have learned to "see themselves as others see them".

Don't drive in another driver's "blind spot". Either pass the other driver or drop back. When you pass another vehicle, get through the "blind spot". Approach cautiously, but once you're alongside, get by quickly.

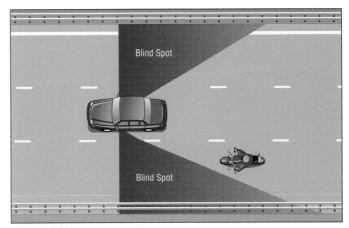

Diagram 5-20

Position for being seen

Look out for intersections

Most collisions between cars and motorcycles happen at intersections. Drivers often have a hard time seeing a motorcycle coming toward them. A vehicle may make a left turn across the motorcycle's path or may pull out from a side street. These are two leading causes of motorcycle collisions at intersections. To cut down your chances of being hit:

1. Approach slowly. If a driver does pull out suddenly, your chances of making a quick stop or a quick turn are better.

2. Move away from the other vehicle as far as you can. If the vehicle is on your right, move to the left. For a vehicle on your left or an oncoming vehicle with a left turn signal on, move to the right.

3. Move away from things that could block the other driver's view. When you approach an intersection, with a car waiting to pull out, move toward the centre of the road so that you're in the other driver's line of sight.

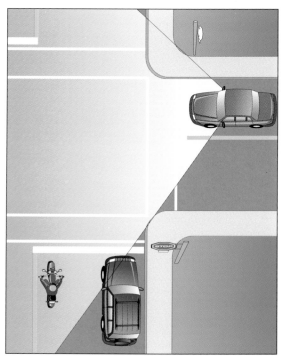

Diagram 5-21

Group riding

The highway is not a place to social-
ize. Motorcyclists riding in groups
do not have any special rights. If
you want to drive with others, you
must do it in a way that does not
endanger anyone or interfere with
the flow of traffic.

Keep the group small

A large group interferes with traffic,
making it necessary for cars to pass
a long line of motorcycles. Also, a
large group tends to be separated
easily by traffic or red lights. Those
who are left behind often do unsafe
things in an effort to catch up. If
your group is larger than four or five
drivers, divide it into two or more
smaller groups.

Keep the group together

Another thing to prevent "catch-up"
is to keep the group together. There
are several ways of doing this.

Plan ahead

If you are the leader, look ahead for
changes. Give signals early so "the
word gets back" in plenty of time.
Start lane changes early enough to
allow everyone to complete the
change.

Put beginner up front

Place inexperienced drivers behind the
leader, where they can be watched by
more experienced drivers.

Check the driver behind you

Let the tail ender set the pace. Use
your mirror to keep an eye on the person behind you. If he or she falls
behind, slow down. If everyone does
this, the group will stay with the tail-
ender.

Know the route

Make sure everybody knows the
route. Then if someone is separated
for a moment, he or she won't have
to hurry for fear of taking a wrong
turn.

Keep your distance

It is important to keep close ranks
and a safe distance. A close group
takes up less space on the highway,
is easier to see, and is less likely to
be separated by traffic lights.
However, it must be done properly.

Don't pair up

Never operate directly alongside
another motorcycle. If you have to
avoid another vehicle or something
in the road, you will have no place
to go. If you have to speak to
another driver, wait until you both
have stopped.

Group riding

Staggered formation

The best way to keep close ranks and yet maintain an adequate distance is through a "staggered" formation. The leader drives to the left side of the lane while the second driver stays a little behind and drives to the right side of the lane. A third driver would take the left position, a normal two second distance behind the first driver. The fourth driver would be a normal two second distance behind the second driver. This formation allows the group to close ranks without reducing following distance and without having drivers drive alongside one another.

Staggered formation can be safely used on an open highway. However, single file should be resumed on curves, during turns, or when entering or leaving a highway.

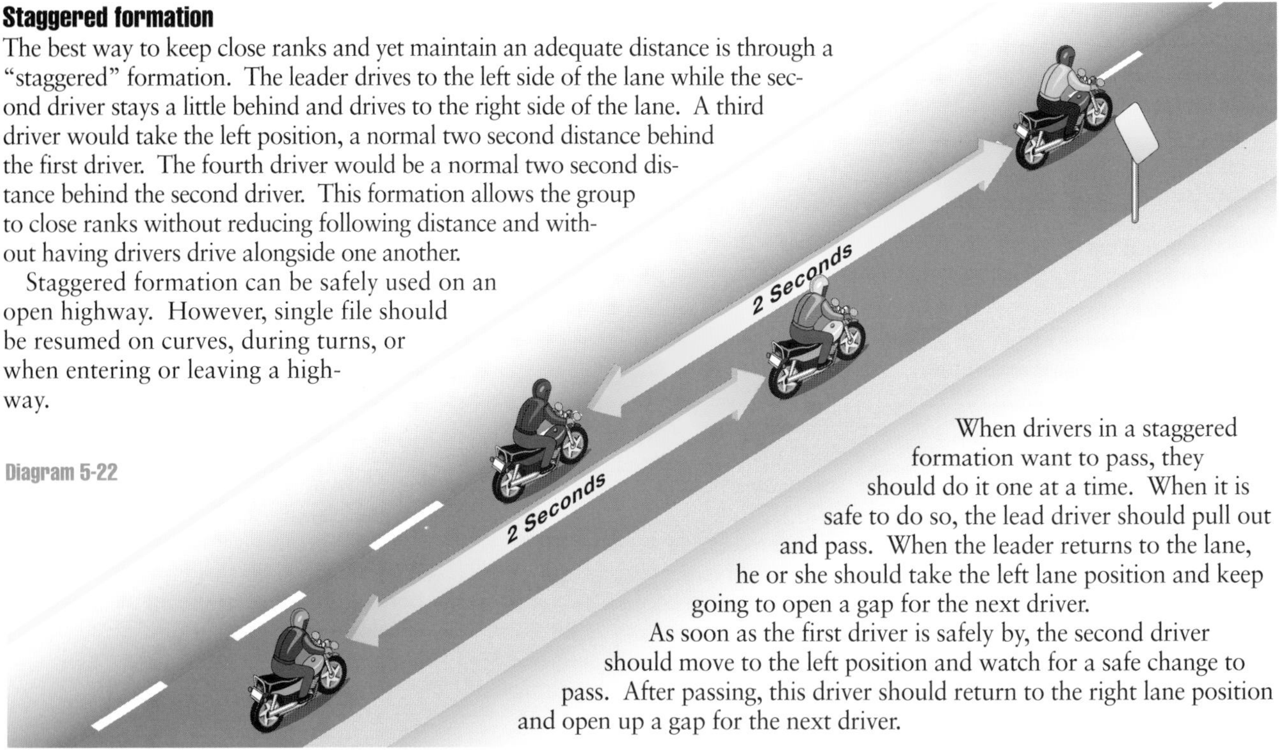

Diagram 5-22

2 Seconds

2 Seconds

When drivers in a staggered formation want to pass, they should do it one at a time. When it is safe to do so, the lead driver should pull out and pass. When the leader returns to the lane, he or she should take the left lane position and keep going to open a gap for the next driver.

As soon as the first driver is safely by, the second driver should move to the left position and watch for a safe change to pass. After passing, this driver should return to the right lane position and open up a gap for the next driver.

Riding at night

Riding at night presents some additional risks.

This is why Class M1 licensed drivers are prohibited from riding at night. The majority of fatal collisions happen after dark.

A major problem for motorcyclists at night is alcohol. Not only are there more drinking drivers on the road to put you at risk, but drivers too often put themselves at risk by drinking. Alcohol reduces your ability to control your own machine, and to anticipate trouble from other drivers.

Another important problem at night is reduced visibility. You cannot see or be seen as well as in the daytime.

Remember to:
Keep your headlight clean and use your high beam

Get all the light that you can. Use your high beam whenever you are not following or meeting another vehicle.

Wear reflective clothing

Also take warmer clothing and a reflective vest if you're going to be out at night.

Reduce your speed

If there is something lying on the road ahead, you will not be able to see it until you are very close to it. If you are going to fast, you may not be able to avoid it. It is important to reduce your speed at night, particularly on roads that you don't know well.

Use the car ahead

If there is a car ahead, you can use it to your advantage. Its lights can give you a better view of the road ahead than your own light. Car taillights bouncing up and down can alert you to bumps or rough pavement.

Increase distance

You cannot judge distance as well at night. You can make up for this by allowing extra distance. Follow at a greater distance from the vehicle ahead. Leave more room on either side of you when riding alongside other vehicles. Give yourself more distance to pass.

55

Handling dangerous surfaces

A motorcycle is balanced on only two wheels. To stay upright, the two wheels must have good traction. Any surface that affects the motorcycle's traction will affect its steering, braking and balance. Any slippery surface reduces your control and increases your chances of falling.

Slippery surfaces

1. Wet pavement, particularly just after it starts to rain and before surface oil washes to the side of the road;
2. Leaves, sand and gravel on hard surfaces such as pavement;
3. Mud, snow, ice;
4. Worn, polished pavement surfaces, particularly when wet.

There are a number of things you must do to operate safely on slippery surfaces:

Reduce speed

It takes a lot longer to stop on slippery surfaces. You must make up for this by going at lower speeds. It is particularly important to reduce speed for curves. Remember, advisory speeds posted on curves apply to good surface conditions.

Avoid sudden moves

Any sudden change in speed or direction can cause a skid on slippery surfaces. Therefore, you should turn, brake, accelerate, and change gears as smoothly as possible.

Use both brakes

The front brake is still more effective than the back brake even on a slippery surface.

Diagram 5-23

Avoid the worst slippery areas

Try to find the best area of pavement and use it.

1. Oil from other vehicles tends to build up in the centre of the lane, particularly near intersections where vehicles slow down or stop. On wet pavement, therefore, it is better to operate in the track created by the wheels of moving vehicles. Some people suggest using the left wheel track all the time.

However, it is not always a good idea. You have to change your lane position for traffic and roadway conditions.

2. Old worn pavements are often polished smooth. When they are wet, they are very slippery. You can see these extra slippery sections if you look for shiny areas on the road surface.

3. Dirt and gravel tend to collect along the sides of the pavement. It is important to stay away from the edge of the road when you make sharp turns at intersections or enter and leave freeways.

4. Certain sections of the road dry out faster after a rain, or snowfall. Try at all times to stay in the best part of the lane.

Unrideable surfaces

It is almost impossible to maintain balance on ice, or wet wooden surfaces. Avoid these surfaces if at all possible. If you can't avoid one of these areas, slow down as much as possible before you get to it. Pull in the clutch and coast across. Pulling in the clutch removes the engine drag from the rear wheel and helps avoid skidding. Stay off the brakes. If necessary use your foot to hold the bike up.

Uneven surfaces

Watch for uneven road surfaces such as bumps, broken pavement, potholes, railroad tracks and construction areas. If the condition is bad enough, it could affect your control of the motorcycle. This is how to handle uneven surfaces:

1. Slow down to reduce the impact.
2. Keep your motorcycle as upright as possible and avoid turning.

3. Rise slightly on the footrests so that you can absorb the shock with your knees and elbows.

Gravel roads

Traction on gravel roads is not as good as on pavement. Some areas are better than others. Stay in the tire tracks away from the loose gravel at the edge of the road.

Construction areas

Drive with extra care in a construction area. Slow down, as the road surface could have ruts, ridged pavement or pavement heaving.

Handling dangerous surfaces

Railroad tracks

It is not usually necessary to change your path when crossing railroad tracks at something less than a 90 degree angle to the road. Be aware of a possible bump, and avoid turning or braking while on the tracks. Remember to check for trains before crossing any railroad tracks.

If a train is approaching, or the signal lights near the track are flashing, stop no closer than 5 m from the nearest rail. Do not proceed until the train has passed and/or the signals have stopped flashing and the barrier has been raised. It is unlawful and dangerous to drive a vehicle through, around or under a crossing gate or barrier while the gate or barrier is closed, or is in the process of being opened or closed.

Diagram 5-24

Diagram 5-25

It **is** advisable to make an angled approach when you want to cross tracks parallel to your path. The same goes for other uneven surfaces like a pavement seam or a gravel shoulder. Don't try to edge across it, but avoid heavy braking or swerving directly over the problem surface.

Grooves and gratings

When you drive over certain surfaces such as rain grooved or slightly rutted pavement, or metal bridge grating, your motorcycle will tend to wander underneath you, or "hunt". Though this may make you feel uneasy, it is not dangerous. Don't try to overpower this motion, or attempt sudden moves. A gentle but firm grip on the bars will see you through.

Riding in bad weather

Rain

Riding in the rain is not fun. You're more likely to be tired and cold. The roadway is slippery, traction may be poor, visibility is reduced and your brakes may be less effective. If you're not prepared for rain, you're sure to be uncomfortable and may be putting yourself at risk.

Here are some tips for riding in the rain:

1. Avoid the worst of it. Sit it out if you're uncomfortable with conditions. Avoid standing water, mud and other dangerous surfaces such as wet metal or leaves.
2. Slow down. Be prepared to stop within the distance you can see clearly. Drive smoothly and avoid heavy braking, swerving and acceleration.
3. Test your brakes periodically. A very light application of the brakes will dry them out if necessary.
4. Try to avoid shiny spots on the road. They are the polished and slippery sections of the pavement, or a puddle. A puddle could hide a large pothole and traction is worse in deeper water.
5. Make yourself visible. Wear bright colours and reflective or fluorescent material.
6. Have good equipment. Make sure you have good tire tread, a good helmet and faceshield plus warm clothing.
7. Wear a one-piece rainsuit to help keep you warm and dry.

You may also have difficulty seeing out of your helmet visor and you may have to lift it up. Some gloves designed for motorcyclists have a chamois surface on the back which you use to wipe water off the faceshield.

Fog

Fog reduces your ability to see road conditions, other drivers, or to be seen yourself. An expert driver will be looking out for fog in low lying areas and by lakes or rivers close to the roadway. Fog may be present at sunrise, sunset, or other times when the air temperature is rapidly changing. As in rain, you will have to wipe your faceshield or lift it up to be able to see out.

In really heavy fog you will only be able to see a few metres. Any time you cannot see farther than your stopping distance, you are riding blind. If there is something stopped on the road, you will hit it. If you slow down enough to be able to stop in heavy fog conditions, you may very well be hit from behind. So either way you lose. The only smart thing to do is find a safe place to stop and wait for conditions to improve.

Riding in cold weather

In winter or in cold weather, even when the road conditions are good other drivers will not be expecting to see motorcyclists. Expert motorcyclists must be even more careful of what other drivers may do and drive more defensively.

The motorcyclist must anticipate sudden changes in the road surface, especially if the temperature is close to or below the freezing point.

A road may be cold and dry in one area, but cold and slippery in another.

Watch for icy or snow-covered patches which may appear on bridges, or shady parts of the roadway; open, wind swept areas and on side roads not completely cleared.

Be alert, the road ahead may appear to be black and shiny asphalt, but don't bet your life on it. Be suspicious. It may be covered by a thin layer of ice known as black ice. Generally, in the winter, asphalt will have a grey-white colour.

If you find that you are unable to avoid riding on a very slippery surface such as ice or snow, slow down as much as possible before you get to it. Pull in the clutch, coast across and stay off the brakes. If necessary use your foot to hold the bike up. On a long section of snow-covered road, try to drive on loose or fresh snow. Hard packed snow has less traction than loose snow.

It is best to avoid riding when you know you are likely to encounter snow or ice.

The other danger of riding in winter is the cold. The cold will affect performance of both driver and equipment. Here are some things to watch for:

1. tire pressure – cold weather lowers tire pressure, check regularly;
2. faceshield fogging which will be worse in cold weather;
3. hypothermia – probably your greatest danger is from fatigue brought on by the cold. If you get cold, your control of the bike will be reduced. Dress in multiple layers. Keep dry. Expose no bare skin to the elements and be alert to your own slowed reactions.

Emergencies

There are times when, in spite of the best intentions in the world, you find yourself facing a situation that needs a quick and effective response.

Studies show that too often unprepared drivers freeze at the controls, or worse, do the wrong thing.

You have at least two options to avoid a hazard on the road – hard braking and swerving.

Braking

Think about the braking tips on page 29. Be prepared to use those techniques in an emergency. Practice quick stops in a safe environment, like a driver training course, to get a feel for it. The goal is to get maximum braking without locking up either wheel.

Confidence in your machine and your abilities is your best ally. Modern motorcycle brakes are very powerful. Some manufacturers now offer antilock braking systems too.

The front brake supplies about three quarters of your braking power, so it is advisable to use both brakes to stop quickly. Pull in the clutch and apply both brakes as hard as you can without locking the wheels.

If either wheel locks, release it momentarily to get the wheel rolling, then re-apply the brakes but not to the point of lock-up.

Emergency steering

Even a quick stop may not be enough to keep you from hitting something in your path. A vehicle ahead might stop suddenly or pull out and partly block the lane. You may be able to steer around an obstacle quicker than you can stop. The only way to avoid a collision could be with a quick turn.

The key to making a quick swerve is to get the motorcycle to lean quickly in the direction you want to turn. It takes practice to do this smoothly and with confidence.

Under normal conditions, you may not be aware that you are in fact pushing forward and down on the right bar to go right, left to go left. This is called push-steering, or countersteering. Be aware of the pressure on the palms of your hands when you turn at usual speeds.

Once you are comfortable with the idea that push-steering describes what is going on, you can practice by pushing harder in order to swerve faster.

Being able to do this well can be very useful in an emergency. It can also give you a welcome feeling of control at all times and add to your enjoyment.

Braking and turning
This involves some risks. It requires
an alert mind and practice.
 Here are some tips for safe collision avoidance.
1. Use the brakes smoothly. The
 back wheel especially is easy to
 lock up. This can cause you trouble while you're leaning.
2. Try to straighten out the motorcycle's path when under heavy braking. Do your braking before your
 turn.
3. Be alert to the dangers of swerving
 into another vehicle's patch.
4. Be aware that you can safely lean
 a great deal more to make a turn
 than you probably think you can.
 Inexperienced drivers too often get
 themselves into trouble in a curve
 because they do not push-steer –
 they do not know the limits of
 their ability to lean.
5. Practice. Take a motorcycle safety
 course.

Getting into a turn too fast
A major cause of serious motorcycle
collisions is running off the road in a
turn or a curve. One of two things
seems to happen:
1. The driver badly misjudges a safe
 speed and gets into the turn much
 too fast, slides off the road and
 crashes into something
2. Inexperienced drivers **think** they
 can't turn sharp enough to make a
 turn; then they brake too hard,
 lock the wheels slide off the road
 and crash.
 Inexperienced drivers sometimes
crash at speeds at which a more
experienced driver could make the
turn.
 Until you learn the cornering limits of your motorcycle, slow down
for turns. Brake before you turn.

Riding over objects
Sometimes you have no choice but
to drive over some object in your
path. Debris on the road, such as a
length of tailpipe may be too close to
you for you to steer around it.
Riding over objects is a lot like riding over uneven surfaces.
 Here is what to do:
1. Hold onto the handgrips tightly so
 that you don't lose your grip when
 the front wheel hits.
2. Keep a straight course. This keeps
 the motorcycle upright and reduces
 the chance of falling on impact.
3. Rise slightly on the footrests. This
 allows your legs and arms to
 absorb the shock and helps keep
 you from being bounced off as the
 rear wheel hits.
 The three steps above let you drive
safely over most of the obstacles you
would find on the highway. It's a
good idea to stop and check your
tires and rims for damage.

Emergencies

Flying objects

From time to time you could be struck by insects, cigarette butts thrown from other vehicles, or stones kicked up by the tires of the vehicle ahead. If you are without face protection you could be struck in the eye or the face. If you're wearing face protection, it could become smeared or cracked making it difficult to see. Whatever happens, don't let it affect your control of the motorcycle. Keep your eyes on the road and your hands on the handlebars. As soon as it is safe, pull off the road and repair the damage.

Animals

Naturally, you should do everything you can to avoid hitting an animal. However, if you are in traffic, don't swerve out of your lane to avoid hitting a small animal. You have a better chance of surviving an impact with a small animal than a collision with another vehicle.

Motorcycles are often chased by dogs. To avoid this, slow down a bit and down shift as you approach the animal. As you reach it, speed up. You will leave the dog behind so quickly that it will usually lose interest. If you find yourself being chased, don't kick at the animal. It is too easy to lose control of the motorcycle.

Mechanical problems

Things that go wrong with the motorcycle itself can also cause emergencies. Critical emergencies can include:

Tire blowouts

If you have a tire blowout, you will need to react quickly to keep your balance.

You cannot always hear a tire blow. You have to be able to detect a flat tire from the way the motorcycle reacts. If the front tire goes flat, the steering will feel "heavy". If the rear tire goes flat, the back of the motorcycle will tend to slide from side to side.

Here is what to do if you have a blowout while riding:

1. Hold the handgrips tightly and concentrate on steering. Try to maintain a straight course.
2. Stay off the brake. Gradually close the throttle and let the motorcycle coast.
3. If it is the front tire that has blown, shift your weight as far back as you can. If it is the rear tire, stay where you are.
4. Wait until the motorcycle is going very slowly, then edge toward the side of the road and coast to a stop.

Stuck throttle

When you try to close the throttle you might find that it won't turn or the engine won't slow down.

Here is what to do:

1. Relax and let up on the throttle.
2. At the same time, pull in the clutch and turn off the engine with the kill switch.
3. If the motorcycle does not have a kill switch, you have a problem.
   (a) You could pull in the clutch and let the engine race until you can stop and turn it off with the key.
   (b) Alternatively, you may be able to leave the clutch out and stop the engine with the brakes.
4. Park the bike until you can get it fixed.

Wobble

Sometimes when going at a fairly high speed, the front wheel can suddenly begin to "wobble" (shake from side to side).

The only thing you can do in a wobble is to drive it out:

1. Firmly grip the handlebars. Don't try to fight the wobble.
2. Gradually close the throttle and let the motorcycle slow down. Don't apply the brakes; it could make the wobble worse. Never accelerate.

Pull off the road as soon as you can stop. If you are carrying a heavy load, distribute it more evenly. If you are at a gas station or have a tire gauge, check your tire inflation. Some other things that can cause a wobble are: (1) a windshield or fairing that is improperly mounted or not designed for the motorcycle, (2) loose steering-head bearings, (3) worn steering parts, (4) a wheel that

is bent or out of alignment, (5) loose wheel bearings, (6) loose spokes, and (7) improper tire tread design.

Chain breakage

Chain failure usually is caused by a worn or stretched chain, which doesn't fit the sprockets properly, or by worn sprockets. When the chain breaks, you'll notice it because you'll instantly lose power to the rear wheels, and the engine will speed up. If the chain locks the rear wheel, you won't be able to disengage it, and it will cause your cycle to skid.

Emergencies

Engine seizure

Engine seizure means that the engine "locks" or "freezes", and it has the same result as a locked rear wheel. However, there is usually some advance warning, giving you time to respond.

Engine seizure is caused by overheating or a lack of lubrication. Without oil, the engine's moving parts will no longer move smoothly against each other, and the engine will overheat. The first symptom may be a loss of engine power. You may also notice a change in the engine's sound.

If your engine starts to seize, squeeze the clutch lever, disengaging the engine from the rear wheel. Pull off the road to the shoulder and stop. Let the engine cool. While you may be able to add oil and restart the engine, it should be thoroughly checked for damage.

Getting off the road

If you have to leave the roadway to check the motorcycle or to rest for a while, here are two important things to do:

Check the roadside

Make sure the surface of the roadside is firm enough to drive on. If it is soft grass, loose sand, or if you are not sure about it, slow down a lot before you turn onto it. Since drivers behind might not expect you to slow down, make sure to check your mirror and give a clear signal.

Pull well off the road

Get as far off the road as you can. A motorcycle by the side of the road can be very hard to spot. You don't want someone else pulling off at the same place.

If you need help, place your helmet on the ground near the road. This is a generally accepted signal among motorcyclists that you could use some help.

Carrying passengers and cargo

If you are a Class M1 licence holder, it is illegal for you to carry passengers. Even with a Class M/M2 licence, you should avoid carrying passengers or large loads until you are an experienced driver. The extra weight changes the way the motorcycle handles, the way it balances, turns, speeds up and slows down.

When you do start to carry a passenger, carry someone who is light before carrying a heavy person.

Here are some guidelines to follow in carrying passengers and cargo:

Passengers

In order to carry a passenger safely, you must do the following:
1. Make certain your motorcycle is equipped to carry passengers.
2. Instruct your passenger before you start out.
3. Adjust to the passenger's weight.

Diagram 5-26

Equipment

To carry passengers, your motorcycle must have:

A proper seat

The seat should be large enough to hold both you and your passenger without crowding. You should not have to move any closer to the front of the motorcycle than you usually do. A passenger should not hang over the end of the seat.

Foot rests

There must be foot rests for your passenger. Without a firm footing, your passenger can fall off and pull you off too.

Protective equipment

A passenger must wear a legal helmet and should have the same type of protective equipment and clothing worn by the driver.

Adjusting for additional weight

You should also adjust the mirrors and headlight to the change in the motorcycle's angle. Have the passenger sit on the seat while you make the adjustments. If you carry a passenger, it is a good idea to add additional air pressure to the tires (check your owner's manual). If the suspension units are adjustable, they should also be adjusted to carry the added weight.

Riding with passengers

When you are carrying a passenger, the motorcycle responds more slowly. It takes longer to speed up, slow down, or make a turn. The heavier the passenger the longer all of these

Carrying passengers and cargo

things take. To adjust for added weight of the passenger, you should:

1. Operate at a somewhat lower speed, particularly on corners, curves, or bumps.
2. Begin to slow down earlier than usual when you approach a stop.
3. Allow a greater following distance and keep more distance between yourself and other vehicles to either side.
4. Look for larger gaps whenever you cross, enter, or merge with traffic.

When you can, warn your passenger when you are about to start moving, stop quickly, turn sharply, or drive over a bump.

Instructing passengers

Don't assume the passenger knows what to do, even if he or she is a motorcycle driver. Provide complete instructions before you start.

A passenger should be told to:

1. Get on the motorcycle after the engine has started.
2. Sit as far forward as possible without crowding you.
3. Hold tightly to your waist or hips.
4. Keep both feet on the footrests at all times, even when the motorcycle is stopped.
5. Lean with the motorcycle.
6. Avoid any unnecessary motion or talk.

Carrying loads

A motorcycle is not designed to carry much luggage. If you must buy luggage, buy a tank bag first, in which the load is central.

Keep the load low

Do not pile loads against a sissy bar or frame on the back of the seat. This will change the centre of gravity and disturb the balance of the motorcycle.

Keep the load forward

Place the load over or forward of the rear axle. Anything mounted behind the rear wheel can affect how the motorcycle turns and brakes. It can also cause a wobble.

Distribute the load evenly

If you have saddlebags, make certain the load in each one is about the same. An uneven load can cause the motorcycle to pull to one side.

Secure the load

Make sure the load is securely fastened and keep the load near the centre of gravity. It's generally not a good idea to tie bundles to the top of the seat.

Check the load

Check the load regularly when you are stopped. Make sure it has not worked loose or moved.

Accessories and modifications

A safe motorcycle can be quickly turned into a menace. If you add accessories incorrectly or make changes in the motorcycle, it can seriously degrade the motorcycle's handling. Here are a few things to avoid:

Highway pegs
These are pegs mounted on the front of the motorcycle to allow the driver to lean back. The pegs may make the driver more comfortable.
The problem is:
1. It takes too long to reach the foot brake in an emergency.
2. Operators don't have the footing needed to maintain balance.

Ape hangers
These are high handlebars that extend above the operator's shoulders.
The problem is:
1. They are illegal in Ontario if they are too high. See page 10.
2. They reduce steering control.
3. They cause your vision to be blocked.

Extended forks
Much longer than standard forks are installed by some drivers for styling.
The problem is:
1. They reduce steering precision.
2.They increase stress on the frame and steering components.

Road race handlebars
Extra low clamp-on type bars are sometimes used by drivers.
The problem is:
They may create discomfort and fatigue and make it harder to make good shoulder checks.

Touring modifications
Unless properly designed and installed, fairings, luggage attachments and containers may overload the bike, change its handling characteristics, or cause a tire blowout.

Maintenance

Weekly motorcycle inspection

Read your owner's manual and save it for future reference.

Inspect the motorcycle carefully and fix things right away. Earlier in this handbook, we described checks that should be made each time you drive. Here are some things to check once each week.

Tires

Check the tread to make sure it is deep enough. You should have no less than 1.5 mm of tread depth left in any groove. If the tread is getting low, buy new tires. Inadequate tread depth will greatly reduce your braking traction on wet roads. If the wear is uneven, have the wheels balanced and the alignment checked. Make sure the air pressure is correct, as many blowouts are due to low air pressure.

Also check for cuts, scrapes, exposed cord, abnormal bumps or bulges, or any other visible tread or sidewall defect.

Coolant

If your engine is water-cooled, check the level.

Battery fluid

Avoid unnecessary problems. Check your battery regularly and refer to your owner's manual.

Drive line

Chain breakage is very dangerous. Maintain the chain and replace it when necessary. Oil the chain and check for wear. Your owner's manual will describe when and how to tighten a chain.

If your bike has shaft drive, check the fluid level.

Diagram 5-27

Wheels

Check both wheels for missing or loose spokes. Check the rims for cracks or dents. Lift the wheel off the ground and spin it. Watch its motion and listen for noise. Also move it from side to side to check for looseness.

Controls

Check the controls for smooth operation. Check the cables for kinks or broken strands. Lubricate the control mechanisms at each end of the cable.

Shock absorbers

Does your motorcycle bound several times after it crosses a bump? Do you hear a "clunk"? If so, your shock absorbers may need to be adjusted or replaced.

Fastenings

Check for loose or missing nuts, bolts, or cotter pins. If you keep the motorcycle clean, it is easier to spot missing parts.

Brakes

If you hear a scraping sound when you try to stop, or if the brakes feel spongy have the brakes serviced immediately.

If your motorcycle has hydraulic brakes, check regularly that the fluid level is high enough.

Muffler

Modifying an exhaust system will create an excessively noisy vehicle. Such a motorcycle can be very annoying to the general public. A motorcycle driver having such an altered muffler may be guilty of an offence.

Now that you have read this far, and the Official Driver's Handbook, could you pass an Ontario Motorcycle Driver's Licence written examination?

Here is a sample question:
When a group of motorcyclists is travelling together the safest way to drive is:
A. Staggered single file?
B. Four abreast?
C. Three abreast?
D. In a group?

Others may ask you about:
– knowledge of motorcycle controls
– proper lane position
– steering control of a motorcycle
– motorcycle equipment requirements
– safety helmets
– carrying passengers or cargo
– handling dangerous surfaces
– "down shifting" of gears
– proper maintenance of your motorcycle
– riding on wet or slippery roads
– and many other subjects contained in this handbook.

So, make sure you have read this and The Official Driver's Handbook carefully and that you understand the information before you take your test.

The Level Two Road Test

Statistics show that new drivers of all ages are far more likely than experienced drivers to be involved in serious or fatal collisions.

To help new drivers develop better, safer driving habits, Ontario introduced graduated licensing in 1994 for all drivers applying for their first car or motorcycle licence. Graduated licensing lets you gain driving skills and experience gradually, in lower-risk environments. The two-step licensing system takes at least 20 months to complete and includes two road tests. Passing the Level Two (M2) motorcycle road test gives you full Class M driving privileges and your Class M licence.

While the Level One road test deals with basic driving skills, the Level Two road test deals with advanced knowledge and skills that are generally gained with driving experience. When you take the test, the examiner will follow you in another vehicle and talk to you by radio through a disposable earphone. The examiner will give you directions. As you complete the driving tasks, the examiner will watch to make sure you successfully perform the actions associated with them.

To help you prepare, this chapter tells you the various tasks and actions that you will be expected to perform in your Level Two road test. This is only a guide. For more information on the driving tasks, read the Official Driver's Handbook.

Left and right turns: The approach

This driving task begins when the examiner tells you to make a left or right turn and ends at the point just before you enter the intersection. Make sure you take the following actions:

Traffic check

Before slowing down, look all around you. Use your mirrors to check traffic behind you and check your blind spot. If you change lanes, remember to check your blind spot.

Lane

Move into the far left or far right lane as soon as the way is clear. If possible, change lanes before you begin to slow down for the turn. Generally, use the left tire track to turn left from a one-lane road and the right tire track to turn left from a two-lane road. A right turn is usually made from the left tire track of the far right lane.

Signal

Turn on your signal before slowing down for the turn unless there are vehicles waiting to enter the road from sideroads or driveways between you and the intersection. Wait until you have passed these entrances so that drivers will not think you are turning before the intersection.

Speed

Steadily reduce your speed as you approach the turn. Downshift into a lower gear as you slow down. Use both front and rear brakes. Do not rely on downshifting only to slow down. Do not drive slower than the speed at which your motorcycle is stable (about 15 km/h) to avoid stopping. At such low speed, the motorcycle must weave to keep upright. Even if you are skilled enough to balance the motorcycle without weaving, the low speed leaves you with only minimum control.

Space

While slowing down, keep at least a two- to three-second distance behind the vehicle in front of you.

If stopped

You will need to do this driving task if you cannot complete your turn without stopping, either because the way is not clear or you face a stop sign or red traffic light. Remember to follow these actions:

Stop   With both front and rear brakes on, come to a complete stop. At the point of stopping, put your left foot down while still keeping both brakes on. Do not put your foot down until you can do so without dragging it along the ground. Once stopped, do not let your motorcycle roll forward or backward. Keep the brake light showing while stopped. When traffic conditions allow, move forward to check that the way is clear or to start the turn. If you have to stop after you have passed the stop line, do not back up.

Tire track   Stop in the correct tire track to block other vehicles from pulling up beside you in the lane. Generally, use the left tire track when turning left from a one-lane road and the right tire track when turning left from a two-lane road. A right turn is usually made from the left tire track of the far right lane. When you stop, you may point your motorcycle in the direction of the turn to let other drivers know you are turning and to keep them from pulling up beside you. If you stop behind a large vehicle, make sure the driver can see you through a side mirror.

Space   When stopped behind another vehicle at an intersection, leave enough space to pull out and pass without having to back up — about one motorcycle length. If the vehicle in front is a large vehicle, leave more space. Leaving this space protects you in three ways: it lets you pull around the vehicle in front if it stalls; it helps prevent you from being pushed into the vehicle ahead of you if you are hit from behind; and it reduces the risk of collision if the vehicle ahead rolls backward or backs up.

Left and right turns: If stopped

Stop line   If you are the first vehicle approaching an intersection with a red light or stop sign, stop behind the stop line if it is marked on the pavement. If there is no stop line, stop at the crosswalk, marked or not. If there is no crosswalk, stop at the edge of the sidewalk. If there is no sidewalk, stop at the edge of the intersection.

Turning

This driving task involves your actions as you make the turn. Remember to do the following:

Traffic check If you are stopped, waiting for a green light or for the way to be clear, keep checking traffic all around you. Just before entering the intersection, look left, ahead and right to check that the way is clear. If there is any doubt about the right-of-way, try to make eye contact with nearby drivers or pedestrians. If it is possible for another vehicle to overtake you while you are turning, check your blind spot before starting to turn. You have not properly checked traffic if another vehicle or pedestrian has the right-of-way and must take action to avoid your motorcycle.

Both feet Keep both feet on the footrests throughout the turn. Do not walk the motorcycle to ease into or around a turn. You are most at risk from other traffic when turning. Keeping both feet on the footrests gives you maximum control when you need it most.

Gears Do not shift gears during the turn. An incorrect gear change during a turn can cause the rear wheel to skid. Generally, not changing gears gives you more control and balance over your motorcycle when it is turning.

Speed Move ahead within four to five seconds after it is safe to start. Increase speed enough that the engine does not stall or over-rev. Make the turn at a steady speed, slow enough to keep full control of the motorcycle while turning, but fast enough to keep your balance and not slow down other traffic.

Wide/short Turn into the corresponding lane on the intersecting road without going over any lane markings or curbs.

Left and right turns: Completing the turn

This driving task completes the turn. It begins when you enter the intersecting road and ends when you return to normal traffic speed. Take the following actions:

Lane
End your turn in the lane that corresponds to the lane you turned from. Generally, you should end the turn in the left tire track. If you are turning left onto a multi-lane road, return to normal traffic speed and move into the curb lane when it is safe to do so. If you are turning right onto a road where the right lane is blocked with parked vehicles or cannot be used for other reasons, move directly to the next available lane.

Traffic check
As you return to normal traffic speed, check your mirrors to become aware of the traffic situation on the new road.

Speed
Return to normal traffic speed by accelerating smoothly to blend with the traffic around you. In light traffic, accelerate moderately. In heavier traffic, you may have to accelerate more quickly. Shift gears as you increase speed.

Cancel signal
Turn off your signal if it does not work automatically.

Stop intersection: The approach

This driving task is done at intersections where you must come to a stop. It begins at the point where you can see the intersection and ends just before you enter the intersection. Be sure to follow these actions:

Traffic check
Before slowing down, look all around you. Check your mirrors and your blind spots.

Speed
Steadily reduce speed as you approach the intersection. Downshift into a lower gear as you slow down, but do not rely on downshifting only to slow down. Use both your front and rear brakes. Do not drive slower than the speed at which your motorcycle is stable (about 15 km/h) to avoid stopping. At such low speed, the motorcycle must weave to keep upright. Even if you are skilled enough to balance the motorcycle without weaving, the low speed leaves you with only minimum control.

Space
While slowing down, keep at least a two-to three-second distance behind the vehicle in front of you.

Stop intersection: The stop

This driving task includes the actions you take while stopped and waiting to move through the intersection. Remember these points:

Stop
With both front and rear brakes on, come to a complete stop. At the point of stopping, put your left foot down **while still keeping both brakes on**. Do not put your foot down until you can do so without dragging it along the ground. Once stopped, do not let your motorcycle roll forward or backward. Keep the brake light showing while stopped. When traffic conditions allow, move forward to check that the way is clear or to start across the intersection. If you have to stop after you have passed the stop line, do not back up.

Tire track
Stop in the correct tire track to block other vehicles from pulling up beside you in the lane. Generally, this will be the same one you used when approaching the intersection. However, if you stop behind a large vehicle, make sure the driver can see you through a side mirror.

Space
When stopped behind another vehicle at an intersection, leave enough space to pull out and pass without having to back up — about one motorcycle length. If the vehicle in front is a large vehicle, leave more space. Leaving this space protects you in three ways: it lets you pull around the vehicle in front if it stalls; it helps prevent you from being pushed into the vehicle ahead of you if you are hit from behind; and it reduces the risk of collision if the vehicle ahead rolls backward or backs up.

Stop line
If you are the first vehicle approaching an intersection with a red light or stop sign, stop behind the stop line if it is marked on the pavement. If there is no stop line, stop at the crosswalk, marked or not. If there is no crosswalk, stop at the edge of the sidewalk. If there is no sidewalk, stop at the edge of the intersection. Stop in a position where other vehicles cannot pull up beside you in the lane.

Driving through

This task includes the actions you take as you drive through the intersection and return to normal traffic speed.
Be sure to follow these actions:

Traffic check   If you are stopped, waiting for a green light or the way to be clear, keep checking traffic all around you. Just before entering the intersection, look left, ahead and right to check that the way is clear. If there is any doubt about the right-of-way, try to make eye contact with nearby drivers or pedestrians. You have not properly checked traffic if another vehicle or pedestrian has the right-of-way and must take action to avoid your motorcycle.

Gears   Do not shift gears crossing the intersection. If you need to, you may shift gears immediately after your motorcycle is moving but before it is well into the intersection. You may also shift gears in an intersection wider than four lanes if not doing so would slow down other traffic. Generally, not changing gears gives you more control over your motorcycle.

Traffic check   As you return to normal traffic speed, check your mirrors to become aware of the traffic situation after you have gone through the intersection.

Speed   Move ahead within four to five seconds after it is safe to start. Return to normal traffic speed by accelerating smoothly to blend with the traffic around you. In light traffic, accelerate moderately. In heavier traffic, you may have to accelerate more quickly. Shift gears as you increase speed.

Through intersection: The approach

This driving task is done at intersections where you may not need to stop. It begins at the point where you can see the intersection and ends just before the entrance to the intersection. Remember to do the following:

Traffic check

As you approach the intersection, look left and right for traffic on the intersecting road. If you have to slow down for the intersection, check your mirrors for traffic behind you.

Speed

Keep at the same speed as you go through the intersection unless there is a chance traffic may cross the intersection in front of you. If so, slow down and be ready to stop. Watch for pedestrians about to cross the intersection, vehicles edging into the intersection or approaching at higher speeds. Using both front and rear brakes, steadily reduce speed as you approach the intersection. Downshift into a lower gear as you slow down, but do not rely on downshifting only to slow down. Do not drive slower than the speed at which your motorcycle is stable (about 15 km/h) to avoid stopping. At such low speed, the motorcycle must weave to keep upright. Even if you are skilled enough to balance the motorcycle without weaving, the low speed leaves you with only minimum control.

Space

Keep at least a two- to three-second distance behind the vehicle in front of you.

Driving through

This driving task includes your actions from the time you enter the intersection until you have crossed it and are returning to normal traffic speed. Remember these points:

Lane

Do not go over lane markings or change tire tracks in the intersection. If your lane is blocked by a vehicle turning left or a vehicle edging into the intersection from the right, slow down or stop instead of pulling out to go around the vehicle.

Gears

Do not shift gears crossing the intersection. If you need to, you may shift gears immediately after your motorcycle is moving but before it is well into the intersection. You may also shift gears in an intersection wider than four lanes if not doing so would slow down other traffic. Generally, not changing gears gives you more control over your motorcycle.

Traffic check

If you slowed down for the intersection, check your mirrors again before returning to normal traffic speed.

Freeway: Entering

This driving task begins on the entrance ramp to a freeway and ends when you have reached the speed of traffic on the freeway. Remember to do the following:

Traffic check

While on the ramp, as soon as you can see freeway traffic approaching from behind, check your mirrors and your blind spot for a space to merge safely. At the same time, watch any vehicles in front of you on the ramp and keep back a safe distance. Continue to divide your attention between watching in front, checking your mirrors and looking over your shoulder to check your blind spot until you can merge safely with traffic.

Signal

If you have not done so already, turn on your signal as soon as traffic on the freeway is able to see your motorcycle on the ramp.

Space

Drive in the left tire track. While on the ramp and merging with freeway traffic, keep at least a two- to three-second distance behind the vehicle in front of you. If traffic is heavy or moving at such a high speed that it is difficult to keep an ideal following distance, change your speed to get the best spacing possible.

Speed

On the ramp, do not drive faster than the safe ramp speed. While in the acceleration lane, increase your speed to match that of freeway traffic. While merging, control your speed to blend smoothly with freeway traffic.

Merge   Merge with freeway traffic in a smooth, gradual movement to the left tire track of the nearest freeway lane.

Cancel signal   Turn off your signal as soon as you have merged with freeway traffic.

Freeway: Driving along

This driving task checks your actions driving along the freeway but not merging, changing lanes or exiting. Be sure to remember the following points:

Traffic check   While driving along, keep checking traffic all around you and look in your mirrors every five to 10 seconds.

Speed   Avoid exceeding the speed limit or driving unreasonably slowly. Whenever possible, drive at a steady speed. Look ahead to where you are going to be in the next 12 to 15 seconds for dangerous situations or obstacles that you can avoid by changing your speed.

Space   Always keep at least a two- to three-second distance behind the vehicle in front of you. If another vehicle follows too closely behind you, give yourself even more room in front or change lanes. Try to keep a space on both sides of your motorcycle and avoid driving in the blind spots of other vehicles. Try not to drive behind large vehicles. Because of their size, they block your view of traffic more than other vehicles. Drive in the correct tire track.

Exiting

This driving task begins when you are driving in the far right lane of the freeway and can see the exit you want to take. It ends when you reach the end of the exit ramp. Remember to do the following:

Traffic check   Before moving into the exit lane, look left and right and check your mirrors. If there is a lane of traffic on your right, such as an acceleration lane from an entrance ramp, or a paved shoulder, remember also to check your right blind spot.

Signal   Turn on your signal before you reach the exit lane.

Exit lane   Enter the exit lane at the beginning of the lane with a smooth, gradual movement. Drive in the left tire track and stay inside the lane markings.

Speed   Do not slow down before you are completely in the exit lane. Once you are in the lane, gradually slow down without causing traffic to pile up behind you. Use both your front and rear brakes to slow down. Downshift as you reduce speed.

Space   Keep at least a two- to three-second distance behind the vehicle in front of you.

Cancel signal   Turn off your signal once you are on the exit ramp.

Lane change

This driving task begins as you look for a space to change lanes and ends when you have completed the lane change. Remember to follow these actions:

Traffic check

While waiting to change lanes safely, look all around you. Divide your attention between watching in front, watching the mirrors, and checking your blind spot. If there is another lane beside the one you are moving into, check traffic in that lane to avoid colliding with a vehicle moving into the lane at the same time as you.

Signal

Turn on your signal when there is enough space for you to change lanes. After signalling, check your blind spot one more time before starting to move into the other lane. Your signal should be on soon enough to give traffic behind you time to react to the signal. If traffic in the lane you are moving into is heavy, you may turn on your signal before there is enough space to change lanes. This will let traffic behind you know that you are looking for a space to change lanes.

Space

Keep at least a two- to three-second distance behind the vehicle in front of you. If there is another lane beside the one you are moving into, be careful not to move in beside another vehicle or into the blind spot of another vehicle.

Change lanes

Change lanes with a smooth, gradual movement into the new lane. Drive in the tire track that gives you the most space between vehicles in the lanes beside you.

Cancel signal

Turn off your signal as soon as you have changed lanes.

Roadside stop: The approach

This driving task begins when the examiner tells you to stop and ends once you have come to a stop. Make sure you take these actions:

Traffic check

Before slowing down, check traffic in front and use your mirrors to check for traffic behind you. If there is a chance of traffic or pedestrians overtaking you on the right, check your right blind spot just before pulling over.

Signal

Turn on your signal before slowing down unless there are vehicles waiting to enter the road from sideroads or driveways between you and the point where you intend to stop. Wait until you have passed these entrances so that drivers will not think you are turning before the stopping point.

Speed

Use both your front and rear brakes to steadily reduce speed as you approach the stop. Downshift into a lower gear as you slow down, but do not rely only on downshifting to reduce your speed. Come to a stop without weaving.

Position

Stop as far as possible off the travelled part of the road. Do not stop where you will block an entrance or other traffic.

Roadside stop: The stop

This driving task includes the actions you take after stopping. Remember to do the following:

Signal   If your motorcycle has four-way flashers, turn off your signal and turn on the four-way flashers.

Park   Depending on the parking surface, position your motorcycle so it will be stable when the kick stand is down. Shift into neutral, or turn off the engine. Put the kick stand down.

Resume

This driving task begins when the examiner tells you to move back onto the road and ends when you have returned to normal traffic speed. Take the following actions:

Start Holding the motorcycle steady, put the kick stand up and start the engine, if necessary.

Signal Turn off your four-way flashers and turn on your left signal.

Traffic check Just before pulling away from the stop, check your mirrors and your left blind spot.

Speed Return to normal traffic speed by accelerating smoothly to blend with the traffic around you. In light traffic, accelerate moderately. In heavier traffic, you may have to accelerate more quickly. Shift gears as you increase speed. Drive in the left tire track.

Cancel signal Turn off your signal as soon as you are back on the road.

Curve

This driving task begins when the curve comes into sight and ends when you have gone completely around it. Follow these actions:

Speed

As you approach, try to determine the safe speed for the curve. To do this, look for clues such as a sign that shows the safe speed, the shape of the curve and the type of road you are driving on. Enter the curve at a safe speed. In a blind curve where you cannot see all the way around it, drive more slowly in case oncoming traffic wanders into your lane or the curve is tighter than you expected. If you need to downshift, do so before entering the curve; do not shift gears in the curve. Not changing gears gives you more control over your motorcycle and reduces the risk of your wheels locking while downshifting. While in the curve, drive at a speed that balances the forces created by turning on the curve. Near the end of the curve, begin accelerating to return to normal speed.

Lane

As you enter the curve, look as far around it as possible. This helps you stay in a smooth line around the curve. If you look only at the road directly in front of you, you are likely to wander back and forth across the lane, forcing you to constantly correct your steering. On a curve with a short sight distance, drive in the tire track where you can see more of the road ahead. If the curve is to the left, use the right tire track. If the curve is to the right, keep as far left as possible while watching for oncoming traffic that might be cutting the curve short. You may also change the tire track you are driving in to create a more gradual curve than if you followed the full curve of the road.

Business section

This driving task is done on straight sections of road where a number of businesses are located. Be sure to do the following actions:

Traffic check

In a business area, there are many places other than intersections where vehicles or pedestrians are likely to enter the road. These include entrances to businesses, institutions and construction sites, as well as pedestrian and railway crossings. At these and any other locations, look left and right to check for vehicles or pedestrians about to enter the road.

Mirror check

While driving along, check your mirrors every five to 10 seconds. Check your mirrors more often in heavy traffic or where vehicles are moving at different speeds.

Lane

Drive in the safest lane for through traffic. This is usually the curb lane. However, if the curb lane is blocked by traffic or there are many curbside hazards, the centre lane may be a safer choice. Drive in the best tire track for traffic conditions. Usually, this is the left tire track in the curb lane and the right tire track in the centre lane. Stay within the lane markings. Look ahead to where you will be in the next 12 to 15 seconds for dangerous situations or obstacles that you can avoid by changing lanes.

Speed

Avoid exceeding the speed limit or driving unreasonably slowly. Whenever possible, drive at a steady speed. Look ahead to where you will be in the next 12 to 15 seconds for dangerous situations or obstacles that you can avoid by changing your speed.

Business section

Space   Keep at least a two- to three-second distance behind the vehicle in front of you. Increase the distance if another vehicle follows too closely behind you. On a multi-lane road, try to keep a space on both sides of your motorcycle and try not to drive in the blind spots of other vehicles. In slow traffic, avoid driving behind large vehicles that block your view of traffic ahead of you. When you stop behind another vehicle, stay back at least a motorcycle length.

Residential section

This driving task is done on straight sections of residential or rural road.
Remember these points:

Traffic check

On a residential road, watch out for entrances to schools, pedestrian crossings, driveways, sidewalks and any other locations where there might be traffic hazards. On a rural road, watch for entrances to residences, farms, businesses and industrial sites. At all these locations, look left and right to check for vehicles or pedestrians about to enter the road.

Mirror check

While driving along, check your mirrors every five to 10 seconds. Check your mirrors more often in heavy traffic or where vehicles are moving at different speeds.

Lane

Generally, drive in the left tire track. If there are no lane markings, stay on the travelled part of the road. On a wide residential street, stay toward the centre of the road away from parked vehicles or pedestrians. Where you cannot see far ahead on the road because of a curve or a hill, drive in a tire track that will keep you from colliding with an oncoming vehicle that is over the centre line. Look ahead to where you will be in the next 12 to 15 seconds for dangerous situations or obstacles that you can avoid by changing lanes.

Speed

Avoid exceeding the speed limit or driving unreasonably slowly. Whenever possible, drive at a steady speed. Look ahead to where you will be in the next 12 to 15 seconds for dangerous situations or obstacles that you can avoid by changing your speed.

Residential section

Space
Keep at least a two- to three-second distance behind the vehicle in front of you. Increase the distance if another vehicle follows too closely behind you. In slow traffic, avoid driving behind large vehicles that block your view of traffic ahead of you. When you stop behind another vehicle, stay behind at least one motorcycle length.

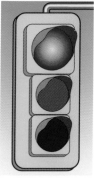

STOP! Did you know there are other books in the official driver information series?

Now you can purchase copies of this official handbook and five others from a retail store, a Driver Examination Office or a Vehicle Licence Issuing Office near you—or you can order them directly from the distributor.

Distribution: **General Publishing Co. Limited**
325 Humber College Blvd., Etobicoke, Ontario M9W 7C3
or by calling (416) 213-1919 ext. 199 or 1-800-387-0141 Fax (416) 213-1917

Prepayment required by cheque or credit card — VISA or Mastercard

QUANTITY			TOTAL
_____	ISBN 0-7778-6141-0	The Official Driver's Handbook	$ 7.95 _____
_____	ISBN 0-7778-6143-7	The Official Motorcycle Handbook	$ 7.95 _____
_____	ISBN 0-7778-4456-7	The Official Off-Road Vehicles Handbook	$ 4.95 _____
_____	ISBN 0-7778-4454-0	The Official Truck Handbook	$ 7.95 _____
_____	ISBN 0-7778-4452-4	The Official Bus Handbook	$ 7.95 _____
_____	ISBN 0-7778-4450-8	The Official Air Brake Handbook	$ 12.95 _____
		Sub-Total	_____
		Plus 12%	_____
_____	Official Road Map of Ontario		$ 2.95 _____

Handbook prices are subject to 7% G.S.T. and 5% shipping costs. Please add 12% to your total purchase. Map is subject to 7% G.S.T., 8% P.S.T. and 5% shipping costs. Please add 20% to your map purchase.

Plus 20% for map _____
TOTAL _____

Payment by   cheque ☐   VISA ☐   Mastercard ☐

Credit Card No. _____   Expiry Date _____

Signature of Card Holder _____

SHIP TO (PLEASE PRINT):

Name: _____

Address: _____

Town/City: _____

Province: _____   Postal Code: _____

Other Official Handbooks for You

Copies of this handbook and others may be purchased from a retail store near you, from a Driver Examination Office, from a Vehicle Licence Issuing Office or from the distributor.

Distribution:

General Publishing Co. Limited
325 Humber College Blvd.,
Etobicoke, Ontario
M9W 7C3

or by calling
(416) 213-1919 ext. 199
or 1 (800) 387-0141

Prepayment required by cheque or credit card — VISA or Mastercard

The Official Driver's Handbook $7.95
ISBN 0-7778-6141-0

The Official Motorcycle Handbook $7.95
ISBN 0-7778-6143-7

The Official Off-Road Vehicles Handbook $4.95
ISBN 0-7778-4456-7

The Official Truck Handbook $7.95
ISBN 0-7778-4454-0

The Official Bus Handbook $7.95
ISBN 0-7778-4452-4

The Official Air Brake Handbook $12.95
ISBN 0-7778-4450-8

All prices are subject to 7% G.S.T. and 5% Shipping Costs. Please add 12% to your total purchase to cover G.S.T. and shipping cost.

NOW THERE ARE MORE WAYS THAN EVER TO EXPRESS YOURSELF!

Personalize your licence plates—with two to eight characters, as well as a great choice of colour graphics. Then you'll really stand out from the crowd.

Turn the page to find out more.

WE'RE HELPING YOU BUILD CHARACTERS.

Now you've got extra choices when creating your personalized licence plate. We've introduced seven and eight characters. So you've got even more to work with—a minimum of two characters and right up to eight. Just think of the possibilities.

Every personalized plate is one of a kind. No one else can have the same plate as yours.

For more information and to order your personalized plates, call 1-800-AUTO-PL8 (1-800-288-6758).

**Or visit our website:
www.mto.gov.on.ca:80/english/dandv/vehicle/personlz.htm**
Or drop by your local Driver and Vehicle Licence Office or one of 60 ServiceOntario kiosks.

Gift certificates are available too.

ONTARIO
BCRE8TVE
YOURS TO DISCOVER

ONTARIO
NOWYOURS
YOURS TO DISCOVER

Graphic licence plates are a hit! And now there are more than 40 choices available. Support your favourite Ontario sports team, community or arts organization, professional group or university. Or select a timeless icon like the loon or trillium.

For a totally unique look, add a colour graphic to a personalized plate with up to six characters.

So express yourself—with colour graphics and personalized licence plates.

For more information and to order your plates, call 1-800-AUTO-PL8 (1-800-288-6758).

Or visit our website: www.mto.gov.on.ca: 80/english/dandv/vehicle/graphic.htm Or drop by your local Driver and Vehicle Licence Office or one of 60 ServiceOntario kiosks.

Gift certificates are available too.

ADD SOME COLOUR WHERE IT COUNTS.